West Coast Support Group

Task Group 96.8

WEST COAST SUPPORT GROUP

TASK GROUP 96.8

KOREA 1950–1953

M.P. Cocker

Whittles Publishing

Published by
Whittles Publishing Limited,
Roseleigh House,
Latheronwheel,
Caithness, KW5 6DW,
Scotland, UK
www.whittlespublishing.com

Typeset by
Samantha Barden

ISBN 1-870325-59-1

By the same author
Destroyers of *the Royal Navy 1893–1981*, Ian Allan
Observers Directory of Royal Naval Submarines 1900–1982, Fredk. Warne
Frigates, Sloops and Patrol Vessels of the Royal Navy 1900 to date, Westmoreland Gazette
Mine Warfare Vessels of the Royal Navy 1908 to date, Airlife Publishing Limited

Printed by
Athenæum Press Ltd, Gateshead, UK

A portfolio of the ships of the Royal Navy, Royal Australian Navy, Royal Canadian Navy, Royal New Zealand Navy, Royal Netherlands Navy, Royal Thai Navy and the Republic of Colombia Navy which all served throughout the Korean War in the West Coast Support Group known as TASK GROUP 96.8 with the authority and resolution of the Security Council of the United Nations.

This volume is published in the 50th anniversary year of the falling silent of the guns which were active from land to sea and sea to land from 1950 to 1953, the period of the Korean War.

THE KOREAN THEATRE (REPRODUCED WITH PERMISSION FROM *EBB AND FLOW,*
NOVEMBER 1950–JULY 1951. CENTER OF MILITARY HISTORY, 1990,
BY BILLY C. MOSSMAN)

Contents

Glossary

AA   anti aircraft
ARC   Republic of Colombia ship
Btry   battery
CAG   Carrier air group
CAP   Carrier air patrol
CAS   Carrier air strike
flak   anti aircraft fire
HMAS   His Majesty's Australian ship
HMCS   His Majesty's Canadian ship
HMDS   His Majesty's Danish ship
HMNS   His Majesty's Netherlands ship
HMNZS   His Majesty's New Zealand ship
HMS   His Majesty's ship
HMTS   His Majesty's Thai ship
LH   Lighthouse
LV   Light vessel
MFA   Mercantile Fleet Auxiliary
MIG   Russian-built Mikoyan and Gurevich fighter aircraft
NK   North Korean
o.a.   over all (length)
POL   petrol oil and lubricants
Pt   point
POW   prisoner of war
RA   Rear Admiral
RAN   Royal Australian Navy
RASCV   Royal Army Service Corps Vessel
RATOG   Rocket Assisted Take Off Gear
RCN   Royal Canadian Navy
RFA   Royal Fleet Auxiliary
RFS   Republic of France ship
RMC   Royal Marine Commando
RN   Royal Navy
ROK   Republic of Korea
ROKN   Republic of Korea Navy
RNZN   Royal New Zealand Navy
R&R   rest and recuperation

SIC	ships in company
sortie	operational flight
Sqdn	squadron (aircraft, armour, ships)
Stormovik	Russian-built Ilyushin Il 2 fighter-bomber
TF	Task force
TG	Task group
TU	Task unit
TE	Task element
USN	United States Navy
USS	United States ship
VA	Vice Admiral
WCSG	West Coast Support Group
WWI	World War I
WWII	World War II
YAK	Russian-built Yakovlev fighter aircraft

Photographs

_____

It is the author's intention to include in this work a photograph of every fighting ship (aircraft carrier, cruiser, destroyer, frigate) and every auxiliary vessel (oiler, naval transport, hospital ship, armament stores carrier, stores issuing ship) which are listed in the index. All sailed in the war zone off Korea and in the many tidal estuaries thereof, maintaining the blockade on the aggressor northern nation by air and sea power and ensuring the ever ready supply whenever required and in varying states of weather of POL, stores, ordnance, ammunition, victualling supplies and enduring the ever constant dangers of floating, moored and bottomed mines, air attack, and enemy gunfire.

Where possible, ship photographs have been obtained in Korean or Japanese waters during the period of the Korean War. However, it has not been possible to obtain prints within this timescale for all the ships listed.

The Naval Archives of Australia, Canada, Colombia, Denmark, France, Netherlands, New Zealand, Thailand and the United States have as usual been very helpful indeed, nor must I omit the assistance received from Korea itself. To all I say thank you, and I have to say it has been more difficult to obtain required photographs of Royal Navy vessels than any other nationality.

(The reader will note that dates/periods of a vessel's arrival in the theatre of operations varies in detail, due to lack of information. However, every attempt has been made to ensure the dates are as accurate as possible. See Appendix 5.)

Ship specifications/technical details
Are listed as at 1950 and mainly from the edition of Janes Fighting Ships of that year.

Acknowledgements

This work was commenced some years ago and in consequence the persons with whom I communicated regarding supply of photographs and information may no longer be with their relevant organisations, so I have decided only to list the latter, in alphabetical order.

Admiralty Material Branch II; Afdeling Maritieme Historie van de Marinestaf, Netherlands; Aldo Fraccaroli, Italy; Australian War Memorial; Devon Commercial Photos Ltd; East Asiatic Co. Ltd., Copenhagen;. Fleet Air Arm Museum; Fleet Photographic Unit, Portsmouth; R.L. Furness Esq.; Government of the Republic of Korea; Imperial War Museum; Museé de la Marine, France; Public Archives of Canada; Royal Fleet Auxiliary Service, Empress State Building, London; Royal New Zealand Navy Archives; Royal Thai Navy Archives; Wright & Logan; Yarrow Shipbuilders Ltd.

I thank my wife Pauline for clerical assistance and my publisher (editor Michael Forder) for their help throughout.

In Memorium to the undermentioned Officers who by their instruction educated this author in Maritime Affairs and the seaward defence of the Realm by service in Peace and War:

Captain D McEwen DSC Royal Navy
Commander R B Chandler OBE Royal Navy
Captain J Mara Merchant Navy
Captain L Richards Merchant Navy
Lieutenant Commander R Wilson RD Royal Naval Reserve
Lieutenant Commander R Browning RD+ Royal Naval Reserve
Lieutenant Commander W H Bethell Royal Navy

With the colleagues of the Royal Naval Mine Watching Service, Royal Naval Auxiliary Service and HM Coastguard Auxiliary Service from 1961 to date including the Stone Frigates HMS *Drake*, HMS *Nelson*, HMS *Pembroke*, and HMS *Raleigh*.

Thanks are due to the Controller, HM Stationery Office for permission to quote from the following:

Our Men in Korea, Eric Linklater HMSO 1952
British Commonwealth Naval Operations in Korea, Admiralty 1953 (unpublished).

Bibliography

Our Men In Korea, Eric Linklater, HMSO 1952.

History of United States Naval Operations: KOREA, James A. Field, Jnr., US Government Printing Office, 1962.

Janes Fighting Ships, various editions, F.T.Jane, Sampson Low and Marston.

The Ships of Canada's Naval Forces 1910–1981, Ken McPherson and John Burgess, Collins, Toronto, 1981.

Allied Escort Ships of World War II, Peter Elliot, MacDonald & Janes, 1977.

Destroyers of the Royal Navy 1893–1981, Maurice Cocker, Ian Allan Ltd, 1981.

Frigates, Sloops & Patrol Vessels of the Royal Navy 1900 to date, M.P. Cocker, Westmorland Gazette, 1985.

Profile Book No. 4. HMS Belfast, John Wingate, DSC, Profile Publications Ltd. 1972.

Aircraft Carriers, David Brown, MacDonald & Janes, 1977.

Fleet Air Arm, J.D.R. Rawlings, Ian Allan Ltd, 1973.

History Of U.N. Forces in Korean War, The Ministry of National Defense War History Compilation Committee, Republic of Korea.

The Army's Navy, David Habesch, Chatham Publishing, 2001.

British Commonwealth Naval Operations in Korea (unpublished), Admiralty 1953.

With the Carriers in Korea, John Lansdown, Crécy, 1997.

Foreword

———

I read with interest Mr Cocker's fascinating report on the operations of the West Coast Support Group and commend it as an excellent and accurate record of events. This conflict received scant media attention at the time and was dubbed The Forgotten War, but this volume helps redress the balance (as does *With the Carriers in Korea*, by John P.R.Lansdown).

My own experience was limited to service in 801 Squadron, flying Sea Furies from HMS *Glory* from November 1952 to May 1953, whereupon I was transferred to HMS *Ocean* and 807 Squadron from May to July 1953. The task allotted to these squadrons was interdiction, which involved destroying bridges and generally interrupting supply to the North Korean front line. During this period I flew only 101 sorties on the ground attack missions and about the same number of combat air patrols in the vicinity of the carrier.

A competition had started between the carriers to see how many operational sorties could be flown in one day, during the hours of daylight. The record stood at 123, held by HMS *Ocean*. Captain Lewin of HMS *Glory* decided that the competition was becoming ridiculous and that to prevent aircrew getting hurt he would demonstrate that HMS *Glory* could equal this number. This was achieved by tea time when we ceased flying for the day but to equal this record, each pilot had flown four or even five sorties in the day!

This is a timely moment for such a book to be published and I welcome it as a useful record of events in this part of the Korean theatre.

Vice Admiral Sir Edward Anson KCB, FRAeS

Introduction

———

This illustrated portfolio is produced as a remembrance of the ships of Task Group 96.8, which saw out between them, three years of largely non-naval warfare. This naval war was able to continue without serious challenge from the navy of North Korea, which comprised small fast attack craft and other vessels which laid covert minefields but did little else.

The vessels taking part had to overcome the ever changing sea, with varying states of tide, ice flows, fog and storms, and in winter arctic conditions. In addition was the ever present threat of enemy air power, which was limited from the start, but nevertheless the ships listed herein contributed greatly to the long campaign by which the Republic of Korea was saved from Communism.

Five years almost to the day of the cessation of hostilities in World War II, once again the victorious Allies (less the USSR) with representatives of the armed forces from many nations which had been freed by the Allies, again took up the arms which they had so recently put aside. This was the first war authorised by the Security Council of the United Nations. That so many nations rallied to the cause, was proof of the worth of that newly-formed organisation. Britain and the older nations of the Commonwealth rapidly legislated by Parliament or otherwise for their reserves to be mobilised, and so largely from Europe and the West came those who would assist the USA liberate the Republic of South Korea from the aggression of its northern neighbour.

Korea

The land mass of Korea is a peninsula projecting southward from North China, being approximately 600 miles in length, by 120 to 160 miles in width, separating the Yellow Sea in the west, from the Sea of Japan in the east.

To the south is the Korea Strait, while the northern land boundary with Manchuria and the USSR is mainly defined by the Tumen and Yalu rivers. Korea is largely mountainous, with about 20% of the land used for agriculture, and the coastline is particularly indented, particularly on the west and south coasts, in which waters lie 3,420 or so islands, many uninhabited and barren. The Korean tides range from nil to over 30 feet at springs, thus giving large estuarial mud flats before and after high water. The climate ranges from arctic to semi-tropical temperatures, according to the season of the year. This then was the terrain and particularly the rivers and seas, through which the ships of the Allies saw action and three years of operations.

Background

―――――

In the beginning

Even in the sixteenth century or as far back as our own medieval period, the country of Korea was a peaceful land under the suzerainty of the Ming Emperors of China. But with the passing decades, visitors of a warlike nature from Japan occupied the land and found it to be much to their liking. By the late nineteenth century, the influence of Japan in Korea practically outweighed that of China, and at the close of the Russo-Japanese War in 1905, the victorious Nippon Empire, with its new and effectively used western technology, was fêted by the European powers. By 1910, Korea somewhat unwillingly, had become a protectorate or vassal state under the dominance of Japan, but without the democratic benefits of protectorates of the British Empire. With the First World War, attention swung to the European, African and Middle-East areas and Great Britain was not displeased to have the Nippon Empire as an ally against the central powers.

At the Peace Conference in 1919 and later, little thought was given to the expansionist programme of Japan, who now regarded Korea as part of her homeland. Up to the Second World War, the Korean economy was stimulated with Japanese aid, factories and railways built, but at the price of the enslavement of a now subject people.

However, in 1943 the United Kingdom and the United States Governments agreed with the USSR at the Cairo Conference, that upon the defeat of Japan, Korea would achieve its long-sought independence. Unfortunately, in 1945 this unhappy nation, like so many others, became divided by agreement, with latitude thirty-eight degrees north being the boundary or border for the Soviet-occupied Korea to the north, and the United States-occupied Korea to the south.

The Security Council

The United Nations Organisation decreed that Korea should be independent by 1950, but only the United States attempted to sow the seeds of democracy for fruition by that year. The USSR was already indoctrinating those under its yoke with Communist ideology, and in 1948, by a show, one party election, had established a Supreme People's Assembly, depending largely on Russian assistance, with some aid from China. The administration of North Korea was so created, together with the formation of armed forces allied to their cause, that the Russians prepared to withdraw their own troops from the north. In consequence, the United States, under UN auspices decided to organize elections in South Korea in the same year, and the resulting

National Assembly was elected in a democratic manner under the leadership of Doctor Syngman Rhee. This result enabled the General Assembly to the United Nations to admit the existence of a *de facto* Southern Republic of Korea in early 1949. This necessitated the need for the withdrawal of all US armed forces personnel, excepting about five hundred military advisors. The South Korean armed forces newly created, comprised infantry and supporting arms, with some motorised units, but not armour. Neither were there any strike aircraft, but there was a small craft Navy of PCS, LCTs, LSTs and other amphibious vehicles.

South Korea again held elections at the request of a United Nations Commission, in June 1950. This action greatly annoyed the Northern regime because of the democratic practices permitted. The leader of North Korea, Kim Il Sung denounced the UN Commission and presumably after conferring with Moscow and Peking, mobilized his forces whilst still calling for a single Korean state. At 0400 local time on 25 June 1950, North Korean forces crossed latitude thirty-eight degrees north and invaded South Korea, at the same time broadcasting that they were repelling an attack from the south, which had emanated from frequent border incursions by southern troops, all of which was a patent lie.

At the Security Council

At the United Nations, the USSR had walked out of the meetings of the Security Council, which met to discuss the invasion and resolved that member states should assist to repel the aggressor. On 30th June 1950, the British Prime Minister, Mr Attlee informed the House of Commons that such Royal Naval forces that were in the Japanese area would be delegated to the defence of South Korea, under the executive command of Vice Admiral G.T. Joy, USN.

The Admiral in command of Royal Naval Units, was Rear Admiral Sir W.G. Andrews, KBE, CB, DSO, RN, holding the office of Flag Officer, Second-in-Command, Far Eastern Station, under ComNavFE, and on the same day, the Governments of Australia, Canada and New Zealand offered their naval forces in the area to the same cause. These Commonwealth vessels were HMS *Triumph* (carrier), *Belfast* (flagship and cruiser), *Jamaica* (cruiser), *Cossack* (leader and destroyer), and HMAS *Bataan* (destroyer), with *Black Swan*, *Alacrity*, *Hart* and HMAS *Shoalhaven* (frigates), and were designated TASK Group 96.8. (Details of the ships and their operational service during their period in Korean waters now follow on their class pages).

On 25 June 1950 the twenty-two Royal Naval ships, including Royal Fleet Auxiliaries, which comprised the Far Eastern Fleet had various tasks. These were the Malayan emergency patrol, to support our forces ashore, the never-ceasing defence of Hong Kong (bearing in mind that the very recently established Communist Government of China, had driven the Nationalist Chinese and its Commanding General Chiang Kai-shek to Taiwan) and was looking with envy at the green paddy fields and prolific buildings seen from the frontier of the New Territories of the thriving sea port and Crown Colony of Hong Kong. And thirdly, to defend such British interests that still remained in mainland China by the continuing patrol of the River Yangtse. However, these ships were allocated to the United Nations command by will of Parliament. The distance from our nearest base was of an order of 1,000 nm, and at this period of the Korean conflict, the ships of the Commonwealth exceeded in numbers the ships of the USN in those waters.

Operational areas for the UN Fleet

It was agreed early on in the Korean War that the east coast would be the prime area for ships of the United States Navy and the west coast for the vessels of the other participating fleets. Both fleets shared the southern coast to a stop line agreed, and ships of any UN nationality operated as required off any part of the coastline of the isthmus of Korea.

HMS Glory, as completed by her builders. Courtesy Harland & Wolff.

HMS Ocean, newly commissioned on the Clyde. Courtesy The Admiralty.

HMS Theseus.

A bow view of HMS Theseus alongside the wharf at Sydney, with a Sea Fury with folded wings parked on the bow. Photograph courtesy of the Imperial War Museum, London. (Neg. no. A31823)

Triumph at anchor, after completion. Courtesy Hawthorn Leslie.

HMS Warrior on builders' trials. Courtesy Harland & Wolff.

Colossus Class Light Fleet Carriers

HMS	COMMENCED	COMPLETED	BUILDER
Glory	1942	1945	Harland & Wolff
Ocean	1942	1945	Stephen
Theseus	1943	1946	Fairfield
Triumph	1943	1946	Hawthorn Leslie
Warrior	1942	1946	Harland & Wolff

Dimensions – there is some variation to a small extent, also on tonnage, speed and shp, etc. Length (o.a.): 693¼/695 feet.　Beam: 80/80¼ feet.　Draught: 23½ feet.

Displacement

Glory and *Ocean*	13,190 tons
Theseus and *Triumph*	13,350 tons
Full load	18,040 tons

Flight deck 690 feet × 80 feet　Arrester wires 8 no
　　　　　　Catapult　　　　　1 no
Hangar 445 feet × 34 feet　Lifts 2 no 45 feet × 34 feet

Armament – gun

Glory, Triumph	*Ocean, Warrior*	*Theseus,*
24 (6 quad) 2 pdr AA	24 (6 quad) 2 pdr AA	24 (6 quad) 2 pdr AA
22 (11 twin) 20 mm AA	7 (single) 2 pdr AA	
10 (10 single) 20 mm AA	12 (12 single) 40 mm AA	21 (21 single) 40 mm AA

Aircraft Fixed & folding wing up to 40
Machinery Geared turbines to 2 shafts giving 39,775/40,339 shp
Speed 23½/24½ knots
Fuel Ship: 3,167/3,196 tons
　　　Aircraft: 98,600 imperial gallons
Complement 1,300 approx

Armour Only 10 mm for magazines and the machinery spaces. A most successful design involving austerity measures.

Korean Service
Deployment and Squadrons

HMS	IN THEATRE	TO	SQUADRONS
Triumph	July, 1950	September, 1950	800, 827
Theseus	October, 1950	April, 1951	807, 810
Glory	April, 1951	September, 1951	804, 812
HMAS *Sydney*	September, 1951	January, 1952	805, 808, 817
Glory	January, 1952	May, 1952	804, 812
Ocean	May, 1952	October, 1952	802, 825
Glory	November, 1952	May, 1953	801, 821
Ocean	May, 1953	July, 1953 (Armistice on 27 July, 1953)	807, 810
Warrior	July, 1950	July, 1953	Ferry carrier, No attached aircraft

All the Carriers listed had brief breaks from operations to rectify minor defects and for R & R of the ships' companies.

HMS *Triumph* was the first RN carrier to take part in the Korean War hostilities, being in theatre when the NK forces invaded the territory of the Republic of Korea on 25 June 1950. Between 2 July and 1 August 1950, her aircraft were airborne for 613 hours, having flown 437 operational sorties. Her aircraft were Seafires and Fireflies, with which she provided carrier air patrols (CAP), and anti-submarine patrols, both of which were important tasks, and during this period she lost two Seafires. *Triumph's* aircraft expended 170,000 rounds of 20 mm cannon shell and 3,400 rockets were fired. She was unfortunate enough to lose two Seafire aircraft during her operations but rescued with her Sea Otter (an amphibious aircraft) a downed American pilot.

On 29 June 1950 together with *Belfast* she proceeded to Okinawa to report to the Commander of the US 7th Fleet which resulted in *Triumph* and the USN carrier *Valley Forge* being together in the 7th Fleet strike force with SIC *Belfast*, *Cossack* and *Consort*. Sorties were launched on 3 July with *Triumph* flying off 21 CAS against targets at Haeju and a second strike after lunch. On the 4th CAS were again launched against targets at Haeju and a similar routine continued. On the 18th *Triumph* launched A/S and CAP in the eastern sea. On the 21st detached with HMS *Comus* to Sasebo for some days but due to a deterioration of the ground situation again put to sea by the 24th heading north. A 'friendly' B-29 shot down an aircraft from *Triumph* but the pilot was rescued unharmed from the sea by her planeguard destroyer. CAS was continued on the 25th for a few days and on the 29th *Triumph* and *Comus* detached for a rest period in Sasebo but both joined the West Coast

Support Group *Jamaica, Kenya, Belfast, Cossack, Cockade, Charity,* HMAS *Bataan,* HMCSs *Cayuga, Sioux, Athabaskan* also HMNS *Evertsen* on 8 August, 1950. By the 15th, her CAS were supporting UN forces on the Naktong perimeter.

On 8th September *Triumph* had two days of operations off the east coast striking and bombarding the coastal railway and NK troop positions near Wonsan, Ulchin and Samchok. On the 12th a landing party was launched from *Whitesand Bay* at Kunsan (a joint US/UK operation). During the Inchon landings from 11 September, *Triumph* with *Jamaica, Ceylon* and *Kenya* and SIC provided CAP, CAS and spotting for naval gunfire at the approaches to Inchon, *Triumph's* aircraft flew 112 sorties and at the completion of this action she was relieved by HMS *Theseus*.

HMS *Theseus* had sailed from Portsmouth on 14 August 1950 to relieve *Triumph*. Seafires had now been replaced by the more powerful Hawker Sea Furys. She left Hong Kong on 2 October and sailed into a typhoon which was an experience for most of her ship's company. She was circled by an unidentified aircraft as she transitted the Straits of Formosa causing hands to action stations but the aircraft quickly disappeared. HMS *Theseus* arrived in theatre on 8 October 1950 and on that day she was off the west coast of Korea commencing a period of intensive operations which included support for the Inchon landings. One of her pilots on CAP was shot down and wounded but recovered by a USN helicopter. Intensive operations followed with a RAS twice off Inchon. The weather was varied, being hot and humid, but as winter approached, ice and snow, mist and fog provided further hazards. During her operational periods, she managed 1,000 accident free deck landings, with at least 50 sorties daily. She expended 6,617 rockets, 1,390 × 500 1b bombs, 84 × 1,000 1b bombs, and 76 depth charges. As for all the carriers, the targets included the usual rolling stock, railway bridges, store dumps, warehouses, tunnels, gun positions, power stations and factories, plus the enemy in the field.

She acquired two Sikorski S51 helicopters manned by USN pilots to replace the Sea Otter amphibian for SAR duties. No fewer than four pilots were rescued from behind enemy lines and four more aircrew were picked up from the sea after ditching. A 'mine carrying barge' was found by a CAG from *Theseus* and was quickly sunk in the south channel to Chinnampo.

The war turned against the UN Command in November 1950 when numbers of Chinese Peoples volunteers in their hundreds, later thousands, came south to assist the NK forces and for the next six months the front line see-sawed north and south of the 38º latitude. *Theseus* had been at Hong Kong but returned to theatre with RA Andrewes. Chinnampo had been taken by the UN but now had to be evacuated which was duly carried out over a three week period with daily CAS from *Theseus* being relieved by the US carriers *Badoeng Strait* and *Sicily* on 27 December 1950.

The war at sea continued as usual. In the New Year of 1951 HMS *Theseus* alternated with the USS *Bataan* on the west coast from 7 January. On the 25th the USS *St Paul* at Inchon was shelled from Wolmi-do but *Theseus* replied with an air strike, also spotting for bombardment from *Ceylon* and SIC. The normal carrier force operations cruised off the Clifford Islands and *Theseus* in the first strikes of the New Year made this her launch area standing out to sea at sunset and returning to sight of land at dawn. There was of course the continuing need to RAS for all the items that keep a ship fighting fit at sea.

In late February, *Theseus* with the USS *Bataan* and SIC were north and close to the ice of the Taedong estuary, *Alacrity* and *Belfast* were inshore bombarding with *Kenya* arriving later and all continuing with the now established routines. April saw *Theseus* and USS *Bataan* off the east coast near the Wonsan area with many air strikes against batteries, facilities, railway and road junctions, bridges and industrial features but on 19 April HMS *Theseus* was relieved by HMS *Glory* and sailed for the UK.

HMS *Glory* arrived in theatre having steamed from the Mediterranean for the first of her three tours. HMS *Glory* with the USS *Bataan* operated off the west coast during the latter part of April, and in May *Glory* with CAP for allied minesweepers was off Cho-do with *Ceylon*, *Kenya* and the USS *Toledo* in company. There were rumours of an NK push to the south near Cho-do where men of the RMC and US Rangers were to raid but the landing was largely unopposed. The weather in the approaching summer was bad with mist, fog and drizzle but *Glory* now had the benefit of longer daylight hours and May/June saw many CAP and CAS. On 11 June *Glory* received contaminated fuel from RFA *Wave Chief* causing *Glory* to leave the line for four days for her tanks to be washed through as a result of this most unusual and unfortunate incident.

On the anniversary of the commencement of the war, 25 June, *Glory* was at maximum effort striking Hwasan-ni north of Sariwon with varied targets and CAP for UN ground forces. NK flak was improving and half of her aircraft had some damage to show on landing back on deck and five aircraft were lost with three aircrew.

In July 1951 a MIG 15 was sighted by *Glory's* CAP lying in shallow water and although 'behind enemy lines' (actually 33 miles north of the Taedong estuary) it was deemed to be better recovered by the UN than the NK and with further CAP from *Glory*, the aircraft wreck was salvaged by a LSU of the USN, covered by HMS *Cardigan Bay* with assistance from *Ceylon* and *Kenya*. Later in the month *Glory* was relieved by the USS *Sicily*, and proceeded to Sasebo later to the west coast again being relieved by *Sicily*. In September two of *Glory's* aircraft force landed at the beach at Paengyong-do but were later recovered, again an LSU was borrowed and with the assistance of *St Brides Bay* and escorted by *Cossack* and *Comus* were transported to HMS *Unicorn*. A final patrol by Glory commenced 21 September being relieved by HMAS *Sydney* on the 30th when she sailed with HMAS *Anzac* for rest and refit to Australia.

HMAS *Sydney* relieved *Glory* at the conclusion of her first tour in September 1951. Her pilots were commended several times for the accuracy of their spotting for bombarding ships, including the battleship USS *New Jersey*. While rearming in

Sasebo for her second patrol she was forced to put to sea on the approach of typhoon Ruth. During the night of 14th October severe damage was suffered by the aircraft on the flight deck, one of the Fireflies being washed over the side. Apart from one short operation on the east coast *Sydney* flew 2,366 sorties in support of Commonwealth troops and repelling NK attempts to occupy the islands on the west coast. She encountered freezing temperatures and typical winter weather for those latitudes, including frequent fog over land targets. On 6th February 1952 she was relieved by HMS *Glory* commencing her second tour.

Glory returned to theatre in Febuary 1952 to the west coast with *Concord* and the USS *Marshall*. The days were short but she continued with CAS against batteries, shipping, store houses, communications and similar targets. In March 1952 her aircraft flew 105 sorties in one day which at that time was a record, later surpassed by the aircraft from HMS *Ocean* with 123 sorties in one day, this later being later equalled by *Glory* herself in her third tour. The same month with *Birmingham* and the USS *Missouri* she struck enemy-held islands opposite Cho-do and Sok-to. On 7 February in bad winter weather four of her Sea Furies were attacked by two MIG 15s north-west of Chinnampo with a similar incident on 23 April. She lost four aircraft 6/12 February with one pilot a fatality. In March she made air strikes on batteries and NK troops near Chinnampo and in April coastal targets near Haeju attracted her attention with spotting for *St Brides Bay*. The following month prior to the end of her second tour she struck communications, buildings batteries and waterways. Her second tour was very similar to the first and in May 1952 she was relieved by HMS *Ocean*.

HMS *Ocean* entered theatre for her first tour in May 1952 and her aircraft were aloft from day one. She struck at Pyongyang on 11 July with 39 sorties on selected targets and her aircraft were attacked by MIGs on the 27th with a further encounter in August involving four incidents over a few days. On 9th August four Sea Furies were attacked by eight MIG 15s resulting in one certain and two possible kills against the MIGs for two damaged Sea Furies with no casualties. This was the only occasion that a piston engined aircraft would shoot down a jet. In August 1952 typhoon Karen caused non-flying weather for a few days with an effect on SIC but Marge caused more trouble.

The 1st Sea Lord Sir Rhoderick McGrigor was visiting theatre during October and witnessed CAS from *Ocean* and bombardments from SIC. On 4th November she rendezvoused with *Glory* off Hong Kong for an exercise. Subsequently 802 and 825 Squadrons were awarded the Boyd Trophy for their achievements in Korea.

Glory's third tour commenced in November 1952 when she relieved HMS *Ocean*.

Although truce negotiations were taking place CAS operations continued as before on the west coast. Snow storms and extreme cold caused some difficulties with starting engines in the mornings. In January and February daily ice reconnaissance patrols were flown to keep the warships blockading the coast informed. From 27th

February to 6th March extreme weather conditions, gales, rain, snow and fog made operations difficult. On Easter Sunday, 5th April 123 sorties were flown, equalling *Ocean*'s record. When she sailed from Sasebo on 19th May she had done three tours of duty, commencing in April 1951 and ending in May 1953, steaming well over 160,000 nm in theatre and her aircraft had averaged 90 sorties daily, providing a total of 12,500.

HMS *Ocean* was the next carrier into theatre relieving *Glory* and carried out many air strikes on the west coast. Commencing 25th May a larger than usual operation commenced with the RN and US naval units on the west coast being under the command of RA Clifford FO2IC. *Newcastle* and USS *New Jersey* were inshore bombarding and on the 28th *Newcastle* was joined by *St Brides Bay* and *Johan Maurits van Nassau* of the Royal Netherlands Navy engaging the recently emplaced batteries on the Amgak peninsula. Later at the end of the month HMS *Modeste*, HMCS *Haida* and HMAS *Culgoa* were on similar inshore bombardments.

On 1st June while at anchor the Sea Furies were RATOGed from the deck to carry out a flypast over the Commonwealth Division in the front line on Coronation Day 2nd June. CAS operations were resumed on 9th June until the armistice was signed on 27th July. At the ceasefire ships in theatre of the Commonwealth included HMSs *Ocean*, *Birmingham*, *Charity*, *Cockade*, *Cossack*, *Whitesand Bay*, the very active HMS *Unicorn* and the depot ship *Tyne* with HMHS *Maine*.

Low intensity patrols and flying training continued until 16th October. During her two tours, her aircraft flew 7,964 sorties, a daily average 76, highest daily 123. Ammunition expenditure 420 × 1,000 lbs, 3454 × 500 lb bombs, 16,490 rockets and 1,500,000 rounds 20 mm cannon shell, with the following results

TARGET	DESTROYED	DAMAGED
Road bridges	115	71
Rail bridges	81	33
Rolling stock	61	73
Motor transport	57	55
Ox carts	172	318
Water transport	102	162
Gun positions/batteries	69	176
Electrical installations	18	37
Enemy killed (pilots' record)	1,000	
Jet fighters MIG 15	1	3

HMS *Warrior*, also a Light Fleet carrier of the Colossus class was employed carrying troops, replacement aircraft and stores from the UK to Singapore and Japan during the course of the conflict.

HMS Unicorn, as operational in WW2 and the Korean War.

HMS *Unicorn*, maintenance and ferry carrier

HMS	COMMENCED	COMPLETED	BUILDER
Unicorn	1939	1943	Harland & Wolff

Displacement	14,750 tons Full load 20,300 tons
Armament – gun	8 (4 × twin) 4" AA
	4 (4 × quad) 2pdrAA
	20 (10 × twin) 20 mm AA
	4 (4 × single) 20 mm AA
Aircraft	Fixed and folding wing – up to 70
Dimensions	Length: (o.a.) 640 feet Beam: 90 feet Draught: 25 feet
Flight deck	600 feet × 80 feet Arrester wires 6 no Catapult 1 no
Hangars	Upper 450 feet × 62 feet Lower 170 feet × 62 feet
	Lifts 2 no 46 feet × 33 feet

13

Machinery	Geared turbines to 2 shafts giving 40,725 shp
Speed	23¾ knots
Range	7,550 nm at 20 knots
Fuel	Ship: 3,157 tons
	Aircraft: 36,000 imperial gallons
Complement	1,200 approx
Armour	Flight deck 2"; crowns 2"; magazine sides 3", bulkheads 1.4"

A one ship class which was most successful.

Korean Service

HMS *Unicorn* was in theatre for the entire period of hostilities of the Korean War. Her purpose during the above period was to carry replacement aircraft and aviation stores from Singapore to Japan where she replenished the operational carrier either from deck to deck, direct transfer or via the advanced operating base at Iwakuni in the Inland Sea of Japan. She also carried a reserve of aircraft and aviation stores up to and in theatre.

Of the five RN carriers she had the largest capacity having an upper and lower hangar with full workshop facilities. She also transported cargo (various, military) stores, ammunition for all three services between Singapore, Hong Kong, Japan and the operational areas.

HMS *Unicorn* was rushed into trooping at the commencement of the conflict by carrying the 1st Bn Middlesex Regt (Duke of Cornwall's Own) from Hong Kong to Pusan to support the shrinking perimeter in the early days of infantry shortage.

She supported the five Light Fleet Carriers on every possible occasion accepting their spare operational aircraft and operating same on many CAG and CAS missions. Additionally with her 8 (4 × twin) 4" DP AA guns she would bombard the coastline on targets offered to her or which she decided to engage independently. Never was one of HM ships more suited to the occasion.

During the Korean War she steamed over 130,000 nautical miles, spent over 500 days at sea, carried more than 6,000 passengers and armed forces personnel and handled at least 600 aircraft.

HMS Belfast at anchor.

Improved Southampton Class Cruiser HMS *Belfast*

HMS	COMMENCED	COMPLETED	BUILDER
Belfast	1936	1939	Harland & Wolff

Displacement	11,550 tons Full load 14,930 tons
Dimensions	Length (o.a.): 613½ feet Beam: 66½ feet Draught: 17¼ feet
Armament – gun	12 (4 triple) LA 6" in turrets at A, B, X and Y positions
	8 (4 twin) DP/AA 4"
	32 × 2 pdr on various mountings
	20 mm AA. The number of weapons and mountings varied
Torpedo Tubes	6 (2 triple) 21" one either beam
Armour	2½" on the turrets with 3" – 5" on the sides. The director control tower was clad in 4".
Machinery	Geared turbines of 80,000 shp to 4 shafts
Speed	32 knots
Fuel	2,260 tons oil fuel
Range	8,000 nm at 14 knots
Complement	710 (peace)

HMS	IN THEATRE	To	FUEL CONSUMED	MILES STEAMED
Belfast	June 1950	August 1950		
	January 1951	September 1952 } 57,000 tons		82,500

Korean Service

HMS *Belfast* proceeded with *Triumph* and destroyers to Okinawa on 29 June 1950 to meet the Commander of the US 7th Fleet, and on 1 July *Belfast*, SIC *Triumph*, *Cossack* and *Consort* joined the 7th Fleet between Korea and Taiwan. The strengthened force proceeded northwards to the western sea and on 3 July *Triumph* and the USS *Valley Forge* commenced CAS to Haeju Man attacking railways, bridges, installations and airfields. Later attacks by the carriers were against Pyongyang, the capital of North Korea. At the conclusion of these air strikes *Belfast* with *Triumph*, *Cossack* and *Consort* detached and proceeded to the southward to join the Support group. It was at this point that separate East and West Coast Support Groups were established with TG 96.5 to the East and TG 96.8 to the West.

The blockade area was designated as north of 37° up to latitude 41ºN on the east coast and up to 39° 30'N on the west coast. On 17 July *Belfast* with *Cossack* was bombarding off the east coast, later patrolling latitude 38° and on the 19/20 with the USS *Juneau* was bombarding off Yongdok with CAS in support of the advance of ROK troops. Later *Belfast* and the USS *Mansfield* withdrew to Sasebo.

Up to the 30th bombardment continued between latitude 38° and Yongdok. At this time RA Andrewes was charged with supervision and tactical command of all non-American United Nations Naval Forces which organization continued throughout the remainder of the Korean War and for which task he acquired a HQ ship berthed at Sasebo (HMS *Ladybird*, see p 59). On 1 August *Belfast* with HMAS *Bataan* was bombarding batteries at Haeju Man and on the 5th *Belfast* with HMS *Kenya* and CAP bombarded suitable targets at Inchon. In February, 1951 *Belfast* navigated the twenty-three mile channel to Wonsan with HMAS *Warramunga*, anchoring off a NK held island with troublesome batteries and silenced them with her secondary armament of 4" guns before engaging targets at Wonsan with her 6" guns. She was constantly involved with the blockade with her not inconsiderable gunfire potential.

By March 1951 on the west coast HMS *Belfast* with *Theseus* and the USS *Bataan* were bombarding and striking at targets near the estuary of the Taedong which was ice covered, the weather including heavy frost. With *Kenya* and SIC *Belfast* continued with her bombardments. RA Scott-Moncrieff took passage to *Belfast* at Inchon onboard HMS *Amethyst* (of Yangtse River fame) on 24 April and on the 28th *Kenya* relieved *Belfast*.

With a refit long overdue and R&R calling *Belfast* steamed south and entered the dockyard at Singapore for a number of weeks.

HMS *Belfast* returned to theatre after refit in Singapore and relieved HMS *Ceylon*. *Belfast* proceeded to the Amgak area and commenced to bombard. On 10th September 1951 *Belfast* was relieved by HMS *Cossack*, five days later *Belfast* was at Inchon on flag duties, and again on 5th/6th October. From October into November *Belfast* was a part of the blockading force and on 9th October with HMCS *Athabaskan* bombarded Kado and Tando on the Chorusan peninsula and NK troop concentrations at Haeju between 18th to 20th October, further action was on 6th November against batteries at Amgak. Earlier HMS *Belfast* during 26th to 30th September had bombarded at Wonsan, Songjin and Chongjin. Again on flag duties she arrived back in theatre from Hong Kong on 20th December and on the 23rd relieved the USS *Manchester* until 7 January 1952 when she was relieved by HMS *Ceylon*.

The Battle of the Islands, of which there are many, was her next engagement, which was due to last 100 days and 76 mm and 105 mm batteries were engaged. The NK forces made their push by loading troops into many junks at the end of November 1951 taking the island of Taewha-do in the Yalu Gulf. HMS *Belfast* during this operation was in company with the USS *Manchester* and *Rochester* and again bombarding the batteries at Amgak. On 20th and 21st November a combined strike took place against Hungnam which is 100 miles north of latitude 38° north, many targets were available and HMAS *Sydney* was to hand with aircraft.

On 15th July 1952 HMS *Belfast* bombarded the island of Changni-do which had hours before been taken by NK forces, on this occasion HMS *Amethyst* was in company. The following day the island was taken back by ROK troops.

Early in August HMS *Belfast* when off the west coast received one hit, she opened fire, silenced the battery and proceeded on her way. In September 1952, HMS *Belfast* left the theatre and proceeded home to the UK. She had been on station at the commencement of the Korean War and had steamed about 82,500 miles expending at least 8,000 6" shells and had been at sea for 404 days.

In 2003 she is the property of the Imperial War Museum, being open to the public daily and is berthed afloat at a jetty in Tower Pool on the River Thames opposite to the Tower of London. HMS *Belfast* saw much action throughout the whole of World War II.

HMS Birmingham.

HMS Newcastle entering harbour, looking a little the worse for wear.

Southampton Class Cruisers

———

HMS	COMMENCED	COMPLETED	BUILDER
Birmingham	1935	1937	HM Dockyard (Devonport)
Newcastle	1934	1937	Vickers Armstrong (Tyne)

Displacement	9,100 tons Full load 12,000 plus tons
Dimensions	Length (o.a.): 591½ feet Beam: 61½ feet Draught: 20 feet
Armament – gun	9 (3 triple) LA 6" in turrets at A, B and Y positions
	8 (4 twin) DP/AA 4"
	16 (8 × twin) 2 pdr pom-poms AA
	22 × 40 mm AA
	15 × 20 mm AA
Torpedo Tubes	(2 triple) 21" on either beam
Armour	1" to 2" turrets with 3"–4" sides and 4" on control tower
Machinery	Geared turbines 75,000 shp to 4 shafts.
Speed	32 knots
Fuel	1,970 tons oil fuel
Complement	810/840 (peace)

HMS	IN THEATRE	TO	FUEL CONSUMED	MILES STEAMED
Birmingham	October, 1952	July, 1953	12,000 tons	18,000
Newcastle	July, 1952	July, 1953	20,000 tons	28,000

Korean Service

HMS *Birmingham* entered theatre in October 1952, unlike *Belfast* she was only armed with nine 6" guns being of a different design and lesser tonnage, however she had served throughout WWII and was fully operational. She arrived in theatre in October 1952 and one of her first duties was to demonstrate her gunnery to the 1st Sea Lord Admiral Sir Rhoderick McGrigor who had made passage on her to the operational zone and viewed the operating of *Ocean*'s aircraft. On 16 November off the west coast she was engaging batteries with SIC *Anzac* and *Crusader*. In the New Year in early January 1953 with typical winter weather, she, with strikes from *Glory* defended the islands of Cho-do and Sok-to from mainland batteries by engaging them together with HMS *Sparrow* and the USS *Missouri*.

She remained on the blockade, bombarding suitable targets on the east and west coasts with the WCSG and units of the US Navy. Further mention is made of *Birmingham* and *Newcastle* in later pages regarding actions with particular ships. At the Armistice she was delegated to supervise evacuations of UN-held islands which had been allocated to the Government of North Korea. HMS *Newcastle* during August 1952 supported raids by Special Forces on land and repulsed attacks on UN-held islands including Tak-son. with SIC *Concord*, HMNZS *Rotoiti*, *Taupo*, HMCS *Crusader* and HMNS *Piet Hein*.

On 23 September *Newcastle* became flagship for RA Clifford CB, FO2IC overseeing the activities of the WCSG and liaison with the USN. The forthcoming winter was not the mildest and ice was prevalent in many areas, but CAS and bombardments continued as part of the island watch and in support of ships of the ROKN. In April 1953 she was off Amgak engaging the strengthened batteries SIC *Cockade*, *Opossum*, *Sparrow*, *Cardigan Bay* and *Whitesand Bay*. Fall of shot was spotted for by CAP from the USS *Baedong Strait* for the bombardments of NK troop concentrations at Haeju, Tanngae and Sunwi-do.

25 May brought a combined shoot under the direction of FO2IC by the USS *New Jersey* and CAS from *Ocean* off the west coast inshore to the north of the Chinnampo estuary.

On 28 May with *Ocean* providing CAS, *Newcastle* and SIC including *St. Brides Bay* and HMNS *Johan Maurits van Nassau* continued bombarding near Chinnampo but NK gunners retaliated necessitating a smoke screen being produced by one of *St Brides Bay*'s boats.

A month later came the Armistice which found *Newcastle* out of theatre.

HMS Jamaica on builders' trials. Courtesy Vickers Ship Builders (Barrow).

HMS Kenya.

Fiji Class Cruisers

———

HMS	COMMENCED	COMPLETED	BUILDER
Jamaica	1939	1942	Vickers Armstrong (Barrow)
Kenya	1938	1940	Stephen

Displacement	8,000 tons Full load 11,730 tons
Dimensions	Length (o.a.): 555½ feet Beam: 62 feet Draught: 20 feet
Armament – gun	9 (3 twin) LA 6" in turrets at A, B and Y positions
	8 (4 twin) DP/AA 4"
	18 × 40 mm on single and twin mountings
Torpedo Tubes	6 (2 triple) 21" one either beam
Armour	2" turrets with 3" – 4" sides and 4" on control tower
Machinery	Geared turbines of 72,500 shp to 4 shafts
Speed	31.5 knots
Complement	730 (peace)

HMS	IN THEATRE	TO	FUEL CONSUMED	MILES STEAMED
Jamaica	June, 1950	October 1950	14,250 tons	31,000
Kenya	June 1950	August 1951	33,000 tons	64,000

Korean Service

HMS *Jamaica* was in the Far East when hostilities commenced on 25 June 1950. By 30 June, *Jamaica* with SIC HMS *Triumph, Belfast, Cossack, Consort, Black Swan, Alacrity* and *Hart*, which with the units of the United States Navy were the commencement of the UN fleet. HMS *Jamaica*, with *Black Swan* proceeded to the east coast, joining a US force, bombarding NK forces on shore. At dawn on 2 July, these ships were engaged in the first naval action of the war, being attacked by six NK fast patrol boats, five were sunk, the survivor heading home. Later in the day, *Jamaica* was bombarding and was hit by a shell from a shore battery. *Jamaica* with SIC *Ceylon*, *Kenya* and *Triumph*, which provided aircraft to report the fall of shot was bombarding off Inchon on the west coast.

By 5 July, *Jamaica*, with USS *Juneau* who she relieved, targeted the coast road close to the sea, destroying bridges, a tank farm and a battery north of Ulchin. They then steamed north demolishing the cliffs which fell and blocked the road, then bombarded the terminal of the coastal railway at Yang Yang setting more oil tanks on fire. On the 8th with HMS *Hart* she was again bombarding the road and traffic thereon however she came under counter fire from a 76 mm piece on shore being hit with the result that she had four of her ship's company as fatalities with eight wounded. She was relieved the same day and proceeded to Sasebo.

On 15 July *Jamaica* was on the coastal patrol and bombarded the industrial area and docks at Kunsan creating fires and extensive damage. The routine continued and in September *Jamaica* was part of the bombarding group at the Inchon landings. On 13 September she used her main and secondary armament to good effect with *Kenya* and the US cruisers *Henderson* and *Rochester* against the Wolmi batteries with spotting from *Triumph's* CAP. *Jamaica* supported the 1st Marine Regt. and as mentioned later shot down an enemy aircraft, having one fatality on board from aircraft strafing. She remained in the vicinity of Inchon until October but having had casualties and damage to her structure she proceeded out of theatre for the necessary R&R and refit.

HMS *Kenya*, with *Triumph* formed part of the bombarding force at Inchon. Her bombardment was observed from a US Navy Corsair, which indicated that her shooting against the batteries was 'one gun blown completely out of its emplacement, two dismounted, a fourth bent with its ammunition on fire' such was the accuracy of her guns. In March, 1951, *Kenya* was unfortunate enough to get her propeller fouled with berthing wire but one of her ship's company cleared the obstruction after one and three-quarter hours underwater. On 28 April 1951, *Kenya* relieved *Belfast* in charge of the blockade patrol, and was in turn relieved by *Ceylon* on 8 May, with SIC HMNS *Van Galen*, HMS *Concord* and HMNZS *Hawea*. On 18 May FO2IC proceeded to Inchon and so missed their part in the patrol of the Han estuary, but for the first time British troops in Inchon were able to see a unit of the Royal Navy, but she sailed on 25 May. She resumed normal patrols with air cover from HMS *Glory*, which had relieved *Theseus* in April. In June 1951 and the first half of July, surface operations consisted of routine patrols and bombardments off the west coast. Ships of this force were HMS *Ceylon*, *Black Swan*, *Cardigan Bay*, *Morecambe Bay*, *Whitesand Bay*, *Mounts Bay*, *Consort*, *Constance*, *Alacrity*, HMAS *Warramunga*, HMCS *Nootka*, HMNZS *Hawea* and *Rotoiti*, and by 15 July they were joined by *Kenya*. In the latter half of the month, *Kenya* with *Cardigan Bay* was detailed to recover a crashed MIG-15 in shallow water south-west of Hanchon, which was a hundred miles north of enemy lines. The task was completed satisfactorily.

The end of July brought operations in the Han estuary and HMS *Ceylon* took charge of this operation and a second in the vicinity of the Haeju estuary. *Glory* gave air cover but was relieved on 5 August by the USS *Sicily*, and *Kenya* relieved *Ceylon*. On 25 August HMS *Kenya* sailed for Singapore to refit and recommission. She had been in the theatre from the outbreak of hostilities, had carried out nineteen patrols and steamed 63,000 miles, also fired 3,386 6" and over a thousand 4" shells, and rescued 10 air crew from the sea.

A summary of the first fourteen days covering the Inchon landings and operations to 30 September 1950 gives the following statistics: ships of the Commonwealth Navies steamed 56,456 miles and *Triumph's* aircraft made 112 sorties. The ammunition expenditure was 2,690 six inch shells, 1,274 lesser calibre and 215,500 rounds of 20 mm cannon shell. The targets in receipt of the above and which were to become so familiar over the three years of the war, were gun emplacements, batteries, ammunition dumps, strong points, armour, troop concentrations and shipping.

The results were, one enemy aircraft downed by naval gunfire, one ammunition dump blown up, two partially damaged, eleven junks sunk, with two damaged, four coasters sunk, and a small freighter damaged, twelve mines destroyed, some NK troops killed and wounded. HMS *Jamaica* had the following items in her log: 'shot down a Stormovik aircraft, which attacked the USS *Rochester*'. *Jamaica* was the first HM ship to enter Korean waters, the first to be in action with enemy E-Boats, the first to bombard in the first bombardment of the war, the first to penetrate the Iron Curtain when she bombarded Yangyang in North Korea, the first to command a combined US and RN force, the first to suffer casualties in the war, the first with HMS *Cockade* to sight and sink mines and she took part in the Inchon landing. On D+3 she was attacked by two Yaks and shot one down but she had one fatality due to strafing.

HMS Ceylon in UK waters.

Uganda Class Cruiser HMS *Ceylon*

HMS	COMMENCED	COMPLETED	BUILDER
Ceylon	1939	1942	Stephen

Displacement	8,718 tons Full load 11,110 plus tons
Dimensions	Length (o.a.): 555½ feet Beam: 62 feet
	Draught: 16½ feet (mean)
Armament – gun	9 (3 triple) LA 6" in turrets at A, B and Y positions
	10 (5 twin) DP/AA 4" with one twin mounting at X position
	40 and 20 mm fitted as per refit
Torpedo Tubes	6 (2 triple) 21" one either beam
Armour	2" turrets with 4" sides and 4" on the control tower
Machinery	Geared turbines of 72,500 shp to 4 shafts
Speed	31.5 knots.
Complement	730 (peace)

HMS	IN THEATRE	TO	FUEL CONSUMED	MILES STEAMED
Ceylon	August, 1950	July, 1952	51,500 tons	86,000

Korean Service

HMS *Ceylon* and HMS *Unicorn* sailed from Hong Kong on 25 August, 1950 with 1,500 troops of the Argyll and Sutherland Highlanders and the Middlesex Regiment. By 29 August they had arrived at Pusan. After a rapid discharge, HMS *Ceylon* joined *Triumph* for spotting as part of the bombarding force at Inchon. HMS *Kenya* who had relieved *Belfast* in charge of the blockade patrol on 28 April 1951 was relieved by HMS *Ceylon* with SIC HMNS *Van Galen*, HMS *Concord*, and HMNZS *Hawea*. On 19 May FO2IC returned to Japan in *Ceylon* after handing over to *Kenya*. In the latter part of June most of the HM ships were on the west coast with HMS *Ceylon* as senior ship. Towards the end of July *Ceylon* was in charge of the operations in the Han and Haeju estuaries, being relieved on 7 August by *Kenya*. Around this time hurricane/typhoon Marge, which brought winds of 110 knots with the consequence that the estuary operations were disrupted. The blockade group consisted of HMS *Ceylon* with SIC *Charity*, *Mounts Bay*, *Morecambe Bay*, HMNZS *Rotoiti* and *Hawea*.

HMS *Ceylon* bombarded in the Amgak area by day and night. On 25 August she landed a raiding party. On 31 August HMS *Belfast* relieved *Ceylon*. The blockade in October and November included HM ships *Belfast*, *Ceylon* now returned to theatre, *Black Swan*, *St Brides Bay*, HMCSs *Cayuga*, *Sioux*, and *Athabaskan*, with HMAS *Murchison* and HMNZS *Hawea*. During 9 to 12 October HMS *Cossack* supported a landing on Sinmi-do which was a large island, and on the 12th *Ceylon* covered the successful withdrawal. The east coast was normally the province of the US Navy, but the tasks being similar to the west coast caused a concentration on counter battery work which Included HMS *Ceylon*. She bombarded at Wonsan, and Songjin and left the east coast on 25 June 1951. On 27 July *Ceylon* relieved *Kenya* but was withdrawn to bombard in the Han river. One of the actions was described as 'the Battle of the Islands' in mid-March, which was estimated to last 100 days, and during which ships of the RN, USN and small craft of the ROK Navy fought many engagements. Many of the islands lie close to the mainland and were of strategic importance to the UN forces. The enemy began his push on 6 November using small craft and junks and Taewha-do in the Yalu Gulf fell to them. On 14 November the *Belfast* was relieved by *Ceylon* with SIC *Whitesand Bay*, *Murchison*, *Hawea* and *Taupo*. During the night of 15 December the enemy attacked Changyang-do and Ung-do, which produced a counter attack by ROK guerillas from Sok-to, covered by HM ships, but the enemy gained the upper hand, *Constance* was hit from a battery at Ung-do but remained operational. The battery was silenced by HMS *Ceylon*.

UN ships included *Belfast*, *Ceylon*, USS *Rochester* and *Manchester*, also *Cossack*, *Cockade*, *Charity*, *Comus*, *Constance*, *Cayuga*, *Athabaskan*, *Sioux*, *Nootka*, *Warramunga*,

Tobruk, Anzac, Bataan, Murchison, Van Galen, Mounts Bay, Whitesand Bay, Cardigan Bay, Alacrity, Rotoiti, Taupo, Hawea and the USS *Taussig, Fletcher, Porterfield, Eversole, Gurke* and *Cumstock*, with rocket ships 401, 403 and 404 and tugs *Apache, Abnaki, Yuma* and *Arikari*.

Air cover was given from HMAS *Sydney* and the USS *Baedong Strait* and later HMS *Glory* and USS *Bairoko*. With cover from the medium guns of the cruisers, the destroyers and frigates closed inshore shooting up strong points and batteries, of which some were mobile and camouflaged. By night the area was illuminated with flares and star shells, there was also a small boat patrol manned by seamen and Royal Marines with ROK and USN personnel. It was intensely cold, with pancake ice, the tugs being needed to cut a way through the ice for the warships to proceed. *Ceylon* with *Belfast* and the USS *Rochester* carried out intense bombardments of batteries on the Amgak peninsula. *Ceylon* with *Constance, Alacrity, Sioux* and the USS *Comstock* responded by bombarding in the Sokto area of the Taedong estuary, being continually shelled by the Amgak batteries.

Off the west coast *Ceylon* supported USS *Bairoko* and together with *Cardigan Bay* bombarded the shore batteries at Wolsa-ri. The usual bombardment routine continued to secure the offshore islands against invasion, until *Ceylon* left the theatre in July.

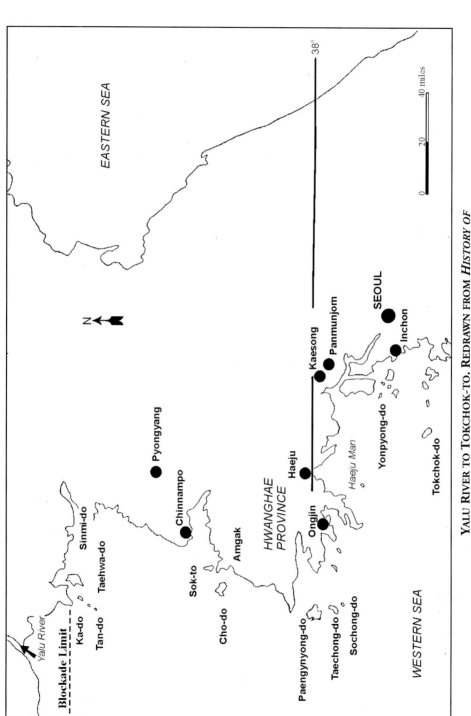

YALU RIVER TO TOKCHOK-TO. REDRAWN FROM *HISTORY OF
UN FORCES IN THE KOREAN WAR (II)*, COURTESY MINISTRY OF NATIONAL DEFENCE, REPUBLIC OF KOREA.

HMS Charity.

C Class Destroyers Ch Group HMS *Charity*

HMS	COMMENCED	COMPLETED	BUILDER
Charity	1943	1945	Thornycroft

Displacement	1,710 tons Full load 2,525 tons
Dimensions	Length: 362¾ feet Beam: 35¾ feet Draught: 10 (mean)
Armament – gun	4 (4 single) DP 4.5" at A, B, X and Y positions
	4 × 40 mm AA
	4 × 20 mm
Torpedo Tubes	4 (1 quad) 21"
Machinery	Geared turbines of 40,000 shp to 2 shafts
Speed	34 knots
Complement	186

HMS	IN THEATRE	TO	FUEL CONSUMED	MILES STEAMED
Charity	August 1950	Armistice*	29,000 tons	126,000

(*see also Appendix 5.)

Korean Service

HMS *Charity* was escorting HMS *Triumph* in August 1950 as part of the west coast blockade. In September she was part of the screen covering the Inchon landings, during which she intercepted an enemy junk which had been laying mines. In the following months *Charity* formed part of the blockading group patrolling the islands on the west coast, on one occasion as far north as the Yalu River.

During continuing operations in the Han estuary typhoon Marge with winds of 110 knots were endured for some days and operations were curtailed until 25th August 1951. On that day a boat party was organised from *Charity* and *Rotoiti* to put ashore a small raiding party in the Amgak area against an NK strongpoint which produced a firefight thus preventing adequate exploration of an enemy gun position. One rating was killed but the remainder returned to their ships under the gunfire of *Rotoiti* and *Charity*.

Off Songjin on 3 September HMS *Charity* relieved *Cossack* and continued bombarding, being relieved by HMAS *Anzac* on 13 September. From July 1951 to February 1952 and later the enemy land forces endeavoured to take a number of islands from UN control and *Charity* was engaged with *Belfast, Ceylon, Cossack, Cockade, Concord, Morecambe Bay* and *Mounts Bay* in the Battle of the Islands for the period of one month. CAS was provided by HMS *Glory*.

In April, 1953 HMS *Charity* with *Cardigan Bay* silenced an enemy battery of 76 mm which menaced the UN-held islands of Cho-do and Sok-to not far from Chinnampo. On 28 May the combined units continued the bombardment of those batteries and at Amgak which had recently been strengthened. *Charity* did two patrols on the east coast and at various times acted as escort destroyer to HMS *Ocean* and *Glory*. At the ceasefire, *Charity* was still in theatre and had steamed 126,000 nautical miles, just 4,000 less than HMS *Unicorn*.

HMS Cockade at sea. Courtesy Yarrow Ship Builders.

HMS Concord. Courtesy The Admiralty.

*HMS Comus preparing to RAS. Photograph courtesy of the
Imperial War Museum, London. (Neg. no. A31692)*

*HMS Consort in the Far East with aft awning rigged. Photograph courtesy of the
Imperial War Museum, London. (Neg. no. A31693)*

*HMS Cossack preparing to RAS. Photograph courtesy of the
Imperial War Museum, London. (Neg. no. A31686)*

*HMS Constance having completed her RAS. Photograph courtesy of the
Imperial War Museum, London. (Neg. no. A31808)*

C Class Destroyers Co Group

HMS	COMMENCED	COMPLETED	BUILDER
Cockade	1943	1945	Yarrow
Concord (ex *Corso*)	1943	1946	Thornycroft
Comus	1943	1946	Thornycroft
Consort	1943	1946	Stephen
Cossack (Leader)	1943	1945	Vickers-Armstrong (Tyne)
Constance	1943	1945	Vickers-Armstrong (Tyne)

Displacement	1,710 tons Full load 2,525 tons
Dimensions	Length: 362¾ feet Beam: 35¾ feet Draught: 10 feet (mean)
Armament – gun	4 (4 single) DP 4.5" at A, B, X and Y positions
	4 × 40 mm AA
	2-6 20 mm AA
Torpedo Tubes	4 (1 quad) 21"
Machinery	Geared turbines of 40,000 shp to 2 shafts
Speed	34 knots
Complement	186 with *Cossack*, 222

HMS	IN THEATRE	TO*	FUEL CONSUMED	MILES STEAMED
Cockade	July 1950	July 1953	28,250 tons	105,500
Comus	July 1950	February 1953	31,400 tons	123,400
Concord	May 1951	July 1953	22,500 tons	95,500
Consort	June 1950	May 1953	29,300 tons	113,000
Constance	October 1950	December 1952	26,000 tons	109,500
Cossack	June 1950	July 1953	29,500 tons	92,300

(*see also Appendix 5.)

Korean Service

HMS *Cockade* in company with HMS *Jamaica* sighted floating mines and destroyed them off the east coast on 7th July, later *Cockade* picked up a USN pilot who had been part of the CAP over the Daido-ko estuary. *Cockade* settled into the familiar routine of patrolling, bombarding and escorting allied shipping.

With *Warramunga*, *Athabaskan*, *Tutira*, *Pukaki*, *Mounts Bay* and *Whitesand Bay* she took part in the Inchon landings. This operation was from 11 September until 14

October and enemy batteries were very prominent at Wolmi-do which was part of the north breakwater of the entrance to Inchon harbour. The destroyers used many rounds of ammunition against Wolmi-do and with further bombardment and CAS the batteries finally fell to the UN forces.

Months later on 7 April 1951 *Cockade* was on the inshore patrol and was approached by a friendly junk which had a US pilot on board who had been shot down 12 weeks earlier, he was glad to be rescued and the junk's occupants were 'revictualled' from *Cockade*. The pilot had been looked after as he confirmed but it was decided to take the Koreans on board in case of possible hostile action if NK sources had learnt of their humane action. During this deliberation she heard an aircraft 'mayday' and proceeded to the position having anchored the junk but an amphibian had claimed the second downed pilot, then another mayday which turned out to be a false alarm so the junk was retrieved and anchored off Techong-do. Night was coming on and as she proceeded, her bow lookout saved her from hitting a floating mine off Songjin. On 30 November/1 December, 1951 *Cockade* was keeping an eye on the ROK-held island of Taewha-do which later that evening was captured by NK troops in junks and sampans who landed and surprised the defenders. *Cockade* sank some of the invading craft and a NK ML. She had personnel ashore who were lost at the time of the landing, an officer and ratings on duties detached from the ship. Enemy battery fire was received and a hit caused a fatality of one rating. Counter battery fire had little result as it was after sunset. Her position was in shoal water and due to the tide she had to withdraw.

Later *Cockade* was part of the screen for the USS *Rendova* operating off the west coast with CAS against the invaders of the previously friendly islands. The UN Command realised the danger of other islands being taken and ROK Marines garrisoned such as seemed liable to be attacked. During the Battle of the Islands *Cockade* sank several NK troop-carrying junks and damaged others probably with loss of enemy life and injuries.

In January 1953 *Birmingham*, *Glory* with air strikes and the USS *Missouri* bombarded the coastline batteries which threatened the UN-held islands of Cho-do and Sok-to and a few weeks later *Cockade* with the USS *Thompson* bombarded industrial buildings and similar targets at Chongjin. She continued with inshore patrols and bombardments and at the ceasefire was still in Korean waters.

HMS *Concord* was in theatre during May 1951 in fact on 28 April she had commenced blockading with *Van Galen* and *Hawea*. By early September she was on patrol in the Yalu Gulf leaving there to join the screen off the Amgak peninsula on 2 September. On 10/11 October with HMAS *Sydney*, *Belfast*, *Comus* and *Cayuga* rocket and gun attacks were made against Kojo and the surrounding-area south of Wonsan. Wonsan was bombarded on 21 October, then giving the same gunnery practice to Hungnam for three days, followed by a few days off Songjin where she was relieved by *Van Galen* on the 31st. The batteries at Hungnam had straddled her at 15,000 yards with a shell 2 cables off her port quarter. The third shot landed in her wash as full ahead was rung down to the engine room.

The next year in April 1952 she was hit, with two ratings killed and four injured off Songjin. During that patrol she had captured five enemy junks and bombarded Chongjin. In August with *Newcastle, Rotoiti, Taupo, Crusader* and *Piet Hien* she gave gunfire support to Tak-son and continued on the inshore patrol.

HMS *Comus* entered theatre in July 1950 and needed a refit but on 5 July was working with the WCSG. On the 21st she was screening *Triumph* for the passage to Sasebo and refit. Back at sea for the 29th again with *Triumph* they left Japan to rejoin the WCSG. Whilst steaming off the west coast in August *Comus* was strafed by an enemy aircraft which caused her some damage, regrettably there was no available CAP. During the spring of 1951, *Comus* with CAP from *Theseus* was off the Chadovy area with *Belfast*, the weather was rough and a rating on *Comus* sustained a compound fracture from the motion of the ship. On 23 April she arrived off Wonsan having been informed of the batteries' activity at Kalma Pondo, which battery rapidly targeted her, causing her to slip her cable as she had to move position quickly. She steamed ahead making smoke, with X and Y guns returning fire. *Unicorn* arrived to salvage two aircraft on the beach at Paengyong-do and *Comus* and *Cossack* escorted her.

The Han river operation was continuing and *Comus* was the first destroyer to navigate those channels, though so strong was the current that she dragged even with two anchors down. She found an anchor berth in more peaceful waters in the river spending three days there and bombarding appropriate targets, from 29 October. She also took part in the Battle of the Islands with *Sydney, Belfast, Concord* and *Cayuga*. Earlier on the 10/11 October with *Belfast* she bombarded Kojo south of Wonsan. With November and winter weather approaching *Comus* was one of the screen for *Sydney* off the west coast and participating in blockade duties. The following year she was patrolling the islands against possible intrusions by NK troops and was joined by *Athabaskan*. The routine continued with bombardments, maintaining the blockade and the frequent requirement to replenish at sea.

HMS *Consort* was in theatre in the beginning in June 1950 and on 1 July was with *Triumph, Belfast* and *Cossack* as units of the 7th Fleet TF 77, patrolling between Korea and Taiwan. The procedures between the two nations' ships were established and on the 7th HMS *Consort* left the 7th Fleet and joined the Commonwealth units off the west coast. Her next task was to familiarise herself with the routines of patrolling, bombarding and enforcing the blockade. She retired from theatre and required a refit with R&R and in July 1951 was back off the west coast, with *Ceylon* as flag ship relieved on the 15th by *Kenya*. In August *Consort* was off the east coast bombarding near Wonsan and was relieved by *Cossack* on the 25th. The next mention is of *Consort* in April 1953 bombarding batteries at Amgak with *Crusader* and showing interest in the coastal railway. Two months later came the ceasefire.

HMS *Constance* arrived in theatre in October 1950 after the Inchon landing and deployed to the WCSG on planeguard duties for *Theseus*, rescuing a rating from the carrier who had by accident fallen into the sea. The following year she was still off the west coast with the usual routines and in December 1951 SIC were the USS *Rendova, Bristol, Collett, Munro, Edmonds* with HMSs *Comus* and *Cockade*. On the night of 15 December the islands of Changyang-do and Ung-do were invaded by NK troops across the mudflats as the tide was out. *Constance* had been bombarding a battery at Ung-do and was hit above the waterline, she continued engaging the enemy and the battery was silenced by *Ceylon*.

Constance also took part in the Battle of the Islands by steaming close inshore shooting up strongpoints and similar targets and she was again hit by shell splinters from mortars at short rangs.

On the 20/21 November 1951 *Constance* with SIC participated in an operation against Hungnam which was an industrial and communications centre one hundred miles north of latitude 38°. RA Scott-Moncrieff flew his flag in *Belfast*, with *Sydney, Tobruk, Sioux, Van Galen* and the USS *Hyman*. There were bombardments with CAP for spotting fall of shot and attacks on the manufacturing area of the city from the US rocket ships, causing much damage to the enemy's war effort and the Hungnam batteries offered little resistance.

In April 1952, *Constance* with *Cossack, Warramunga* and *Bataan* were bombarding off Songjin and noted the increased response from the the guns on shore.

Later in the year, *Sydney* was operating off the west coast and included in her screen were *Constance, Alacrity, Whitesand Bay, Van Galen* and USS *Edmonds*. The routine continued and *Constance* retired for refit and R&R.

HMS *Cossack* was one of the first destroyers active in theatre in the Korean War. On 1 July *Cossack* with *Belfast* and *Consort* joined the US 7th Fleet also known as TF77 patrolling between Taiwan and Korea but later the same day headed for the west coast. On the 17th *Cossack* with *Belfast* was bombarding coastal targets including the advancing NK force adjacent to the coast. The following day *Cossack* again with *Belfast* was patrolling near latitude 38° and on 5 August steamed into the approaches of Inchon with *Belfast, Kenya* and *Charity* to bombard all relevant targets with spotting from CAP of the USS *Sicily*. On 10 September *Cossack* relieved *Belfast* and the following month 9/12 October *Cossack* with *Belfast* and *Athabaskan* supported a landing on Sinmi-do and bombarded Kado and Tendo. Earlier on 25 August *Cossack* relieved *Consort* off Wonsan and on entering harbour was straddled by a battery registered on the entrance, which was then dealt with by return fire. Two days later she steamed north and and took charge of the Songjin units but was relieved by *Charity* on 3 September. HMS *Cossack* took part in the Battle of the Islands where bombardment was the order of the day.

The following year, 1951, *Cossack* patrolled off Yong-do for three nights targeting the coastal railway by shooting up three trains and damaging seven others.

The Han operations followed and *Cossack* with *Charity* was screening the USS *Sicily* having relieved *Glory*. It was *Comus* and *Cossack* who escorted the LSU which had salvaged two aircraft from *Glory* which had made forced landings on the beach at Paengnyong-do to HMS *Unicorn*. In 1953 *Cossack* on 19 June was off Tanchon bombarding the coastal railway with the USS *Gurke* and later off Pukchong, she had some success causing destruction and death on shore. At the ceasefire she was still on patrol but enjoyed a R&R two days later at Kure.

HMS Black Swan. Photograph courtesy of the Imperial War Museum, London. (Neg. no. A28787)

Black Swan Class Frigate

HMS	COMMENCED	COMPLETED	BUILDER
Black Swan	1938	1941	Yarrow

Displacement	1,470 tons Full load 1945 tons
Dimensions	Length: 299½ feet Beam: 37½ feet Draught: 8¼ feet (mean)
Armament – gun	6 (3 twin) DP/AA 4" at A, B and X positions
	8 × 2 pdr AA
	2 × 20 mm AA
Machinery	Geared turbines 3600 shp to 2 shafts
Speed	19¾ knots
Fuel	240 tons oil fuel
Complement	180

HMS	**IN THEATRE**	**TO**	**FUEL CONSUMED**	**MILES STEAMED**
Black Swan	June, 1950	November, 1951*	6,000 tons	41,000

(*see also Appendix 5.)

Korean Service

HMS *Black Swan* with *Jamaica* proceeded to the east coast and was involved in the first naval action of the war on 2 July when she and SIC were attacked by 6 NK fast patrol boats of which five were sunk and one survived to attack another day.

Gunfire support was given by *Black Swan* at the Inchon landings in September 1950 and SIC were HMNS *Evertsen*, HMS *Cockade* and HMNZS *Tutira*. The rest of the year1950 brought further bombardments, patrols and a continuation of the blockade.

In late April 1951 *Black Swan* picked up one pilot who on his first flight from HMS *Glory* had had to ditch. *Black Swan* was in charge of the Songjin siege from early May until the 20th but was then relieved by *Nootka*. She had also captured an armed junk and taken same as prize to a friendly port with subdued crew and passengers from the junk as POWs. From June to October it was routine bombardments, patrols and blockading, but in October she entered the Han river with HMNZS *Rotoiti* and bombarded the north bank synchronising with strikes from *Rendova's* aircraft. Both ships concentrated on the coastal road and bridges that day and the following day hit a tank farm and battery north of Ulchin aiming at the cliffs to block the road with rubble. They concluded matters by bombarding the coastal railway terminal at Yangyang. *Black Swan* bombarded for two or three days then being relieved by *St Brides Bay*, on 6 October. On 9 November 1951 she left theatre for the UK. She had expended at least 4,500 rounds of 4" ammunition, steamed at least 41,000 nm and at one period was at sea for 60 days.

HMS Alacrity. Photograph courtesy of the Imperial War Museum, London. (Neg. no. A28781)

HMS Amethyst. Photograph courtesy of the Imperial War Museum, London. (Neg. no. A30154)

HMS Crane at Valetta, October 1951. She has single 40mm on the bridge wings and on the quarterdeck, with a twin 40mm aft of the funnel. Courtesy Wright & Logan.

HMS Hart at Valetta, April 1957. She has single 20m AA port and starboard of the bridge. Courtesy Wright & Logan.

HMS Modeste at sea, December 1952. She has single 40mm either side of her bridge and on the quarterdeck, with a twin 40mm either beam aft of the funnel on sponsons. Courtesy Wright & Logan.

HMS Opossum. Photograph courtesy of the Imperial War Museum, London. (Neg. no. A29817)

HMS Sparrow at Valetta, September 1952. She is not fitted with the quarterdeck 40mm. Courtesy Wright & Logan.

Modified *Black Swan* Class Frigates

HMS	COMMENCED	COMPLETED	BUILDER
Alacrity	1943	1945	Denny
Amethyst	1942	1943	Stephen
Crane	1941	1943	Denny
Hart	1942	1943	Stephen
Modeste	1943	1945	HM Dockyard Chatham
Opossum	1943	1945	Denny
Sparrow	1944	1946	Denny

Displacement   1,430/1,490 tons   Full load   1880/1975 tons

Dimensions   Length: 299½ feet   Beam: 38½ feet   Draught: 8¾ feet (mean)

Armament – gun   6 (3 twin) DP/AA 4" at A, B and X positions
                        8 × 2 pdr AA
                        2 × 20 mm AA

Machinery	Geared turbines 4,300 shp to 2 shafts
Speed	19¾ knots
Fuel	240 tons oil fuel
Complement	180

HMS	IN THEATRE	TO*	FUEL CONSUMED	MILES STEAMED
Alacrity	June 1950	February 1952	7,900 tons	69,300
Amethyst	February 1951	June 1952	7,400 tons	78,000
Crane	March 1952	July 1953	6,400 tons	37,200
Hart	June 1950	March 1951	3,900 tons	41,000
Modeste	April 1953	July 1953	2,400 tons	17,300
Opossum	December 1952	April 1953	2,750 tons	24,000
Sparrow	December 1952	June 1953	1,850 tons	10,750

(*see also Appendix 5.)

Korean Service

HMS *Alacrity* was in theatre on 30 June 1950 and commenced to patrol and blockade off the west coast from 5 July, preventing seaborne trade from entering enemy waters. Sometime later she was working with units of the USN off the east coast and obtained valuable experience of this. From 21 March to 25 April of 1951, she had engaged numerous, targets and expended 2,290 rounds of 4" shell plus lesser calibres.

With air strikes from USS *Bataan*, from 27 February 1951 *Alacrity* with USS *Carmick* and 2 ROKN PFs steamed north and entered the ice-covered estuary of the Taedong with CAP from the carriers spotting for bombardments against enemy batteries on the shores of the river. Between 21 March to 25 April she expended 2290 rounds of 4" ammunition plus other of lesser calibres. On 13 April when off Yo-to Island she fouled her cable but with good seamanship this was cleared. From June she was on the routine tasks in the Sokto area with *Ceylon*, *Constance*, *Sioux* and the USS *Comstock* bombarding where she was straddled by shore batteries. Later with *Warramunga* she was on the same task off Songjin but her good fortune continued to hold.

In February 1952 *Alacrity* again came under fire off Songjin receiving six hits, minor damage and no casualties. On the night of 24 March the enemy seized an island between Cho-do and Sok-to and she and *Ceylon* were heavily shelled by the Amgak batteries whilst she was repelling the enemy attack.

Later in the year she was a unit of the screen for *Sydney* together with *Constance*, *Whitesand Bay* and *Van Galen* and continued the normal blockade routine.

HMS *Amethyst* arrived in theatre in April 1951. She was already a veteran of WWII and the Yangtse Incident having been under gunfire many times. Her arrival brought RA Scott-Moncrieff to Inchon for an inspection of the WCSG where he joined *Belfast*. In the meantime *Amethyst* joined with the established routine and with *Nootka* patrolled off Inchon and the Han estuary. On 14 September she embarked RA Scott-Moncrieff again to enter the Han for a 'run over the course'. By the 21st the NK batteries opened up and a ROKN Hydrographic ML with *Amethyst* was hit but the frigate was only splashed. On 7 October she relieved HMNZS *Rotoiti* for the usual tasks and in June 1952 was alongside at Inchon for a visit of FM Lord Alexander of Tunis, Chief of the Defence Staff. Other RN ships in harbour included *Ocean*, *Belfast* and *Consort*. Admiral Sir Guy Russell CinCFEF also visited theatre at this period. The 15 July brought an invasion of Changni-do and *Belfast* with *Amethyst* bombarded these intruders on what had been a UN-held island but the following day ROK troops retook it with much loss and casualties to the enemy. The following month typhoon Karen created bad conditions at sea but not as much as Marge the previous year. The routine continued but *Amethyst* left theatre for the UK later that year.

HMS *Crane* entered theatre in March 1952 and remained still off the Korean coast until the cease-fire celebrations. She commenced bombarding on 16 March off Ho-do which had been under enemy attack. Unhappily she received one hit at long range which caused minor damage but no casualties. She settled into the routine and by the Armistice in 1953 was involved in the evacuation of the population of certain islands which the UN had decided to allocate to North Korea. She was relieved of this task by HMCS *Iroquois* and later returned to the UK and the Suez affair.

HMS *Hart* was in theatre in June 1950 and deployed as escort to US ships carrying service personnel from Japan to Korea. In early July on the 7th she relieved *Black Swan* near Chumunjin and the following day with *Jamaica* was bombarding the coastal road to halt the enemy from proceeding to the southward. USS *Swenson* and the two RN vessels later proceeded south towards Pohang arriving for the 9th. *Hart* entered into the blockade routines and returned to the UK mid-1951.

HMS *Modeste* arrived in theatre in May, 1953 and joined the inshore line, with HMAS *Culgoa* and HMCS *Haida* bombarding gun positions and batteries at Amgak and off Chinnampo and such duties as required until the cease-fire. She was also operational in the Red Sea for the Suez operation in 1956.

HMS *Opossum* arrived in theatre by January 1953 and was quickly into the skills of bombarding installations near Haeju and batteries at Tanngae and Sunwi-do. On 9 February she, together with *Crane* and HMNZS *Hawea* hunted a sonar contact classified as a submarine, but several salvoes of Squid produced no result.

HMS *Sparrow* was in theatre by January 1953 and quickly inducted into the blockade routine. She bombarded batteries at Haeju that month but received minor damage fortunately without casualties. Later In April with *Newcastle*, *Cockade*, *Cardigan Bay*, *Whitesand Bay* and *Opossum* she was inshore bombarding at Amgak close to Sok-to Island. She continued with these routine tasks until the cease-fire.

HMS Cardigan Bay. Photograph courtesy of the Imperial War Museum, London. (Neg. no. A30789)

HMS Morecambe Bay at Valetta. Besides her twin 4" she has a canvas-covered Hedgehog at 'A' position, and a number of 20mm AA weapons.

HMS Mounts Bay.

HMS St Brides Bay.

HMS Whitesand Bay at sea with her paying off pendant. She has a single 40mm on the quarterdeck. Other light AA weapons appear to have been dismounted. Courtesy Wright & Logan.

Bay Class Frigates

HMS	COMMENCED	COMPLETED	BUILDER
Cardigan Bay (ex *Loch Laxford*)	1945	1945	Hy Robb
Morecambe Bay (ex *Loch Heilen*)	1944	1949	Pickersgill
Mounts Bay (ex *Loch Kilbirnie*)	1944	1949	Pickersgill
St Brides Bay (ex *Loch Achillty*)	1944	1945	Harland & Wolff
Whitesand Bay (ex *Loch Lubnaig*)	1944	1945	Harland & Wolff

Displacement	1,600 tons Full load 2,530 tons
Dimensions	Length: 307½ feet Beam: 38½ feet Draught: 12¾ feet
Armament – gun	4 (2 twin) DP/AA 4" at B and X positions
	6 × 40 mm AA
	2 × 20 mm AA

49

Anti submarine	1 or 2 hedgehogs			
Machinery	Triple expansion 5,500 ihp to 2 shafts			
Speed	19 knots			
Fuel	720 tons			
Range	9,500 nm at 12 knots			
Complement	157			

HMS	IN THEATRE	TO*	FUEL CONSUMED	MILES STEAMED
Cardigan Bay	November 1950	July 1953	14,000 tons	62,000
Morecambe Bay	October 1950	July 1953	15,200 tons	84,300
Mounts Bay	August 1950	June 1953	15,300 tons	88,000
St Brides Bay	December 1950	June 1953	13,000 tons	72,000
Whitesand Bay	August 1950	July 1953	13,500 tons	67,000

(*see also Appendix 5.)

Korean Service

HMS *Cardigan Bay* was in theatre off the west coast in June 1951 and on 20 July given the special task of recovering a crashed MIG-15 in shallow water about 100 miles north of latitude 38° off Hanchon. With an attendant USN landing craft and *Cardigan Bay*'s motor boat the task was completed over two tides with no enemy activity to speak of and with CAP from *Glory*. The ships in company to complete the operation bombarded a NK gun position about 15 cables away.

On 26 July HMS *Cardigan Bay* with HMAS *Murchison* and ROKN PF 62 entered the wide reaches, fast tides and switching channels of the Han river. HMNZS *Hawea* was the radar picket. Entry was by the western channel and the frigates steamed up river with caution to anchor by nightfall. At daybreak being spotted and advised by the CAP from USS *Sicily* they navigated the channel between the mudflats to gun range of the northern shore moving to the eastern channel. Targets appeared to be few and far between but much hydrographic information was obtained. HMS *Mounts Bay* relieved *Cardigan Bay* and HMNZS *Rotoiti* relieved *Morecambe Bay* with *Murchison* then having a week of R&R. The frigates rotated and continued bombarding and surveying the river channels until November. Later HMS *Cardigan Bay* was present at the Battle of the Islands with her sister ships *Mounts Bay* and *Whitesand Bay*.

In April 1953 HMS *Cardigan Bay* and SIC *Newcastle*, *Cockade*, *Opossum*, *Whitesand Bay*, *Condamine*, *Athabaskan* and *Hawea* were patrolling inshore near Haeju and Sunwi-do. *Cardigan Bay* engaged an enemy battery which threatened the nearby islands. At the Armistice HMS *Cardigan Bay* was still on the gunline off the coast of Korea.

HMS *Morecambe Bay* was in theatre on 12 June 1951 off the east coast close to Chongjin and Wonsan bombarding traffic on the coastal railway for 15 days expending over 1,000 4" shells. Targets included roads, permament way, rolling stock, locomotives – diesel and steam, repair gangs, repair cranes and tampers and ballast wagons, also rail stacks and signalling items. The railway was damaged and cut, bridges broken and collapsed, buildings damaged and NK troops wounded and killed. She trapped a locomotive in a tunnel then collapsed the other entrance, coaches were set ablaze. The gunnery action was maintained day and night with the night illuminated by starshell and flares. By her actions the coastal railway was crippled with NK front line troops being short of manpower, provisions and ammunition.

In June/July 1951 she was off the west coast patrolling and bombarding. After typhoon Marge HMS *Morecambe Bay* was with *Mounts Bay* and *Hawea* returning to the river Han for the action described with *Cardigan Bay* above.

On 9 March 1952 HMS *Morecambe Bay* when off Chongjin had her wireless aerials shot away by an enemy battery. Later between 23 to 29 September 1952 *Morecambe Bay* investigated the many junks using the Han river and visually surveyed the channels which had been navigated in late 1951. June 1953 saw her active off Chinnampo bombarding batteries and troops in field detachments with the USS *Thompson*, the batteries returned the fire but there were no hits or casualties. In a matter of weeks she saw out the Armistice off the coast of Korea.

HMS *Mounts Bay* was in theatre by September 1950 and was deployed in the protective screen at the Inchon landings. She returned to the west coast again during June/July 1951 and met Marge like many other of the frigates, relieving *Cardigan Bay* in the Han river and rotating with the SIC. She continued to monitor the occupation of the many islands mostly by guerillas from each side, some changing hands with numbers of small craft going to and fro in warlike operations.

On 22 July 1951 *Mounts Bay* was on the east coast and relieved *Morecambe Bay* in company with *Ceylon*. HMAS *Sydney* was the carrier at this period on the west coast and provided CAP for *Mounts Bay* and *Ceylon* during their bombardments. In August 1952 HMS *Mounts Bay* with *St Brides Bay* and *Condamine* were off the east coast, she relieved *St Brides Bay* and some days later attracted fire from an NK battery being hit five times with one fatality and some casualties. In returning the fire she hit one gun and continued on patrol.

By November she was back amongst the islands off the west coast and created inshore patrols towards the end of the year, the idea being to keep the approaches to Amgak and Chinnampo illuminated during the dark hours. *Whitesand Bay* was also involved in this scheme. The patrol was code named Smoking Concert and whichever frigate had the senior officer, was Sitting Duck.

By April 1953 she was on inshore patrols with the usual tasks hitting a gun cave (hidden battery) with HMNZS *Kaniere* off Chinnampo. She continued with the Commonwealth force until the Armistice off the Korean coast.

HMS *St Brides Bay* was in theatre by September 1951 and escorted a landing craft with the task of recovering two of *Glory's* aircraft which had force landed on the beach at Paengyong-do. A team from HMS *Unicorn* was embarked and saw to the aircraft being recovered for repairs to *Unicorn*, *Cossack* and *Comus* were escorts. She was employed in the blockade during October /November with *Belfast*, *Ceylon*, *Black Swan*, *Cayuga*, *Sioux*, *Athabaskan*, *Murchison* and *Hawea*. *St Brides Bay* also contributed to the operation in the Han river, and was interrupted by Marge. On 6 October, *Black Swan* was relieved by *St Brides Bay* and *Amethyst* relieved *Rotoiti*.

In July 1952 *St Brides Bay* with *Mounts Bay* and *Condamine* were patrolling the east coast between 4/6 August in conjunction with the USSs *Carmick* and *John R. Pierce* to deny the enemy use of the coastal railway. Six box cars loaded with timber and sand were derailed. *St Brides Bay* watched over the wreck from the morning of the 5th until the morning of the 6th, firing with close range weapons and main armament to deter those who attempted to clear the track. She was relieved by the *John R. Pierce*, which during the afternoon engaged an NK field battery that retaliated, with hits causing casualties and damage. The US destroyer had no surgeon on board and *St Brides Bay* tranferred her own medical team.

St Brides Bay was relieved by *Mounts Bay* having become the twelfth Common-wealth ship which had been hit by enemy shore battery fire within the previous nine months. Damage to the ship was unimportant and she maintained her patrol. In April 1953 HMS *St Brides Bay* bombarded gun positions in the Chaerwonj area, with spotting of fall of shot by *Glory's* aircraft. By 28 May British and Netherlands warships including *Newcastle*, *St Brides Bay* and *Johan Maurits van Nassau* with CAP from *Ocean* bombarded new gun positions on the north shore of the Chinnampo estuary and the Amgak peninsula, returned fire was received and a motor boat from *St Brides Bay* laid a smoke screen. *Newcastle* engaged with her main and secondary armament withdrawing into the smoke screen, with *St Brides Bay* continuing the bombardment until out of range. She continued with the usual patrolling and blockade duties and was at sea when the Armistice came into effect.

HMS *Whitesand Bay* was in theatre by 11 September 1950, her duties were escorting and screening the vessels off Inchon. During the Inchon landings a party of Royal Marines carried out a number of raids with a diversionary attack at Kunsan with American special forces. Off the west coast in June/July 1951, *Whitesand Bay* was patrolling and bombarding keeping the blockade complete. The entry into the River Han involved fourteen ships with *Whitesand Bay* joining in early November. This brought the one hundredth day since entry into the river and its charting had commenced. Ships involved were *Black Swan*, *Cardigan Bay*, *Comus*, *Morecambe Bay*, *Mounts Bay*, *St Brides Bay*, *Murchison*, *Hawea*, *Rotoiti* and *Taupo*. They made seventy-four passages, going aground fourteen times, and took eighty-five thousand soundings in the course of surveying the twenty-six miles of channel, and thirty-three buoys were laid. 15,370 rounds of ammunition of various calibres were expended on the enemy.

During June *Whitesand Bay* was operating off the east coast with *Ceylon*, bombarding at Wonsan and Songjin, she was relieved by HMCS *Huron*. Towards the end of the year, *Whitesand Bay* was again on blockade duties and in the Han river estuary with *Murchison* continued to bombard the north bank by day and night. The two ships with *Hawea* patrolled for periods of between four to seven days, becoming very familiar with the Han estuary. *Whitesand Bay* was involved in the Battle of the Islands which has been mentioned previously. Off the west coast HMAS *Sydney* provided CAP for *Constance, Alacrity, Whitesand Bay, Van Galen* and the USS *Edmonds*. The last six months of the war included inshore patrols, with *Newcastle, Hawea, Athabaskan, Condamine, Cardigan Bay, Cockade, Opossum* and *Whitesand Bay*. On 17 April she was hit by five rounds from a shore mounted 76 mm gun, fortunately with minimal damage. She counter fired 51 rounds against the battery, with a further 40 rounds three days later, at the same position. At the Armistice HMS *Whitesand Bay* was at sea off the Korean coast.

HMS Alert entering Singapore Naval Base. Courtesy R.L.Furness.

Modified Loch Class Frigate HMS *Alert*

HMS	COMMENCED	COMPLETED	BUILDER
Alert (ex *Dundrum Bay*, ex *Loch Scamadale*)	1944	1946	Blyth Ship Builders

Displacement	1,600 tons Full load 2,440 tons
Dimensions	Length: 307½ feet Beam: 38½ feet Draught: 12¾ feet
Armament	2 (1 twin) DP/AA 4"
	2 × 40 mm AA
	4 × 3 pdr saluting guns
Machinery	Triple expansion 5,500 ihp to two shafts
Speed	19 knots
Fuel	720 tons oil fuel
Range	10,000 nm at 11 knots
Complement	160

HMS	IN THEATRE	TO
Alert	August 1950	October 1950
	October 1951	October 1951

Korean Service

HMS *Alert* had been employed as the despatch vessel to the Commander-in-Chief Far East Station. She was used as headquarters ship until the purchase and fitting out of HMS *Ladybird* in August 1950. On 27 September 1951 HMS *Alert* brought C-in-C FE VA the Hon. Sir Guy Russell to Sasebo. During her service in the Korean war HMS *Alert* consumed 2,500 tons of fuel oil and steamed 5,000 miles.

HMS Tyne at Valetta. Note her 'A' and 'B' gun mountings are cocooned. Photograph courtesy of the Imperial War Museum, London. (Neg. no. A33145)

Destroyer Depot Ship HMS *Tyne*

HMS	COMMENCED	COMPLETED	BUILDER
Tyne	1938	1941	Scotts Ship Builders

Displacement	11,000 tons Full load 14,600 tons
Dimensions	Length (o.a.): 623 Beam: 66 feet Draught: 20¾ feet
Armament – gun	8 (4 twin) DP 4.5", positions A, B, X & Y
	8 (2 quad) 2 pdr AA
Machinery	Geared turbines to 2 shafts giving 7,500 shp
Speed	17 knots
Fuel	1,400 tons of oil fuel
Complement	520 but with accommodation for 1,000 overall

HMS	**IN THEATRE**	**TO**
Tyne	April 1953	July 1953

Was equipped with two furnaces, foundry, machine shops with milling and grinding machines, and a bakery with daily output of 25,000 lb. of bread.

Korean Service

HMS *Tyne* was the depot ship on the Far East station with a capability for ship repairs berthed at Sasebo close to the dry docks. Maintenance to armament, radio, ASDIC, weapons repairs and machinery maintenance were all within her remit. She also had accommodation, with many cabins and living spaces which were used by the Commonwealth Naval Force. She consumed 2,500 tons of oil fuel and steamed 5,000 miles in theatre.

*HM Hospital Ship Maine at her buoy in Korean waters. Photograph courtesy of
the Imperial War Museum, London. (Neg. no. A31694)*

Hospital Ship HMHS *Maine*

HMHS	COMPLETED	BUILDER
Maine (ex *Empire Clyde*, ex *Leonardo da Vinci*)	1925	Ansaldo San Giorgio

Gross tonnage	7,515 as built
Dimensions	Length: 429½ feet Beam: 52 feet
Machinery	Double reduction geared turbines to two shafts

Notes: was taken as a prize from the Italians at Kismayu in Italian Somaliland on 14
February 1941, and was employed by the Ministry of War Transport, but in 1948 was
converted for the Admiralty into a hospital ship and renamed HMHS *Maine*.

HMHS	**IN THEATRE**	**TO**
Maine	June 1950	February 1952
	May 1952	June 1953

Korean Service

At the commencement of the Korean War, HMHS *Maine* was at Kobe, Japan and arrived at Pusan in July, 1950. She undertook eight voyages, Pusan to Japan with 1,849 casualties of the forces at war. However it became apparent that she was not suited to this climate, having poor ventilation and the engine and boiler rooms amidships, nevertheless her staff treated many wounded including 2,115 US personel and up to 1,006 cases of surgery were completed.

HMS Ladybird as deployed. Photograph courtesy of the Imperial War Museum, London. (Neg. no. A31830)

Headquarters Ship HMS *Ladybird* (ex *Wusueh*)

Gross Tonnage	3,400 as built	
Dimensions	Length: 295 feet Beam: 46 feet	

HMS	IN THEATRE	TO
Ladybird	September 1950	April 1953

Korean Service

Was an ex-commercial Yangtse passenger ferry purchased in August 1950 to take over as HQ ship from HMS *Alert* for the period of the Korean War. She was moored alongside in Sasebo until relieved by HMS *Tyne* in April 1953.

Mercantile Fleet Auxiliary MFA *Choysang*
(ex *Empire Witham*, ex *Aeolus*)

———

Gross tonnage   1,923 as built
Dimensions   Length: 282 feet   Beam: 44 feet

Note: was taken as a prize at Kiel in May, 1945 by units of the RN.

Korean Service
Employed during the Korean War as an MFA.

Ships of the Royal Fleet Auxiliary
and Mercantile Fleet Auxiliary

———

Records of the voyages of the ships of the RFA and MPA are sparse but an extract from the *British Commonwealth Naval Operations in Korea* Staff paper is reproduced here.

The work of supplying the fleet continued with its usual efficiency but almost unnoticed, yet without the valuable support of the above in all weathers, warships of the United Nations Fleet could not continue with their missions.

An example of the type of work carried out by *Wave Chief* in one routine period was 66 Replenishments At Sea of fuel and aviation fuel at sea, taken on by ships of the Royal Navy, Royal Canadian Navy, Royal Australian Navy, Royal New Zealand Navy, United States Navy and Royal Netherlands Navy. *Wave Chief* was one of the Blue Ensign ships which had fuelled, armed, clothed and fed the United Nations Fleet in Korean waters.

Of seventy fleet auxiliaries operated by the Admiralty, about a third contributed to the Korean War effort by transporting fuel and other military supplies to the Far East and distributing these supplies to ships in the Korean theatre of operations. In less than two years over 90,000 tons of fuel of various grades were replenished at sea and a further large quantity was supplied to ships in port.

These fuelling at sea operations were known as a RAS, the sailor's term for replenishment at sea, which involved the passing of bulky fuel hoses from the tanker to the receiving ship, sometimes having a receiving ship either beam of the supplier and on occasion a further receiving ship astern of the supplier, while all steamed at 10 to 12 knots. Often, the task was carried out in the competitive spirit of a sporting event and ships' companies endeavoured to better the record set by RFA *Wave Knight* and HMCS *Athabaskan*, when only 105 seconds elapsed from firing the pilot line across until the pumping of fuel commenced. To those of the Commonwealth Fleet, RFA *Fort Rosalie* was probably the most well-known RFA. She operated in the area for eighteen months at least returning to the UK in late 1952.

During her service off Korea she supplied a large proportion of the ammunition used by the Commonwealth ships and with onboard teams of specialists inspected, repaired and replaced guns of all calibres worn out by repeated bombardments.

Almost 9,000 tons of bombs, rockets, and small arms ammunition plus associated ordnance, pyrotechnics and miscellaneous items were supplied by her.

The *Fort Rosalie* was relieved by *Fort Sandusky* which had been carrying on the essential work demonstrated by her predecessors in the area and in the historic traditions of the Royal Fleet Auxiliary Service.

RFA Abbeydale at Valetta, April 1951. Courtesy Wright & Logan.

RFA Echodale in light draught. Courtesy Royal Fleet Auxiliary.

RFA Eaglesdale in light draught. Courtesy Royal Fleet Auxiliary.

Oilers, Dale Class

RFA		**COMPLETED**	**BUILDER**
Abbeydale	Type 2	1936	Swan Hunter
Echodale	Type 1	1941	Hawthorn Leslie
Eaglesdale	Type 1	1942	Furness Ship Builders

Displacement	*Echodale*) *Eaglesdale*)	17,000 tons	*Abbeydale* 17,210 tons
Deadweight **Capacity**	*Echodale*) *Eaglesdale*)	12,000 tons	*Abbeydale* 11,650 tons
Dimensions	*Echodale*)	Length: 483 feet Beam: 59 feet Draught: 27½ feet mean	
	Eaglesdale) *Abbeydale*	Length: 481½ feet Beam: 62 feet Draught 27½ feet mean	

64

Machinery	*Echodale*)	B & W diesel giving 3,500 bhp to one shaft
	Eaglesdale)	
	Abbeydale	Doxford diesel giving 4,000 bhp to one shaft
Speed	*Echodale*)	11½ knots
	Eaglesdale)	
	Abbeydale	11½ knots
Complement	*Echodale*)	40
	Eaglesdale)	
	Abbeydale	40

RFA Birchol in loaded state. Courtesy Royal Fleet Auxiliary.

RFA Oakol with cargo part-discharged. Courtesy Royal Fleet Auxiliary.

Oilers, OL Class

RFA	COMPLETED	BUILDER
Birchol	1946	Lobnitz
Oakol	1946	Lobnitz

Displacement	2,670 tons Deadweight capacity 1,050 tons
Dimensions	Length: 232 feet Beam: 39 feet Draught: 15¾ feet
Machinery	Triple expansion to 1 shaft giving 1,140 ihp
Speed	11 knots
Complement	26

RFA Brown Ranger down to her marks. Courtesy Royal Fleet Auxiliary.

RFA Green Ranger under way. Courtesy Royal Fleet Auxiliary.

Oilers, Ranger Class

—

RFA		COMPLETED	BUILDER
Brown Ranger	Type 1	1940	Harland & Wolff (Govan)
Green Ranger	Type 2	1941	Caledon S B & E (Dundee)

Displacement	Type 1	3,313 tons	
	Type 2	3,417 tons	
Dimensions	Type 1	Length: 365¾ feet	Beam: 47 feet
		Draught: 20 feet	
	Type 2	Length: 355¼ feet	Beam: 47 feet
		Draught: 20 feet	
Machinery	Diesel engine to 1 shaft giving 2,750 bhp		
Speed	Type 1	12 knots	
	Type 2	12 knots	

Oilers of this class had the funnel offset to port.

RFA Wave Chief ready to RAS. Courtesy Royal Fleet Auxiliary.

RFA Wave Conqueror in light state. Courtesy Royal Fleet Auxiliary.

RFA Wave Knight in light condition at her buoy. Courtesy Royal Fleet Auxiliary.

RFA WaveLaird with HMS Kenya for RAS. Photograph courtesy of the Imperial War Museum, London. (Neg. no. A31837)

RFA Wave Monarch making smoke. Courtesy Royal Fleet Auxiliary.

RFA Wave Premier. Courtesy Royal Fleet Auxiliary.

RFA Wave Prince at anchor. Courtesy Royal Fleet Auxiliary.

RFA Wave Regent at anchor. Courtesy Royal Fleet Auxiliary.

RFA Wave Sovereign in light condition. Courtesy Royal Fleet Auxiliary.

Oilers, Wave Class

RFA	COMPLETED	BUILDER
Wave Chief (ex *Empire Edgehill*)	1946	Harland & Wolff (Govan)
Wave Conqueror (ex *Empire Law*)	1943	Furness Ship Builders
Wave Knight (ex *Empire Naesby*)	1945	Laing
Wave Laird (ex *Empire Dunbar*)	1946	Laing
Wave Monarch	1944	Harland & Wolff (Govan)
Wave Premier	1946	Furness Ship Builders
Wave Prince (ex *Empire Herald*)	1946	Laing
Wave Regent	1945	Furness Ship Builders
Wave Sovereign	1945	Furness Ship Builders

Displacement	16,476/16,483 tons average Deadweight capacity 11,900 tons
Dimensions	Length: 492½ feet Beam: 64¼ feet Draught: 28½ feet
Machinery	Double reduction geared turbines of 6,800 shp to one shaft
Speed	15 knots

Korean Service

RFA *Wave Premier* on 9 June 1951 inadvertently pumped aviation fuel to HMS *Glory* which proved to be contaminated by corrosion in one of her internal pipes. HMS *Glory* returned to Kure to drain and cleanse her tanks two days earlier than planned.

RFA Fort Charlotte at a buoy. Courtesy Royal Fleet Auxiliary.

RFA Fort Langley. Courtesy Royal Fleet Auxiliary.

RFA Fort Rosalie making way. Courtesy Royal Fleet Auxiliary.

RFA Fort Sandusky at her buoy. Courtesy Royal Fleet Auxiliary.

Fleet Supply Ships, Fort Class

———

RFA	COMPLETED	BUILDER
Fort Charlotte	1944	WCSB (Vancouver)
Fort Langley	1945	Victoria Mchy
Fort Sandusky	1944	United S.Y.
Fort Rosalie	1944	United S.Y (Montreal)

Displacement	9,788 tons Full load 1,3820 tons
Dimensions	Length: 424¾ feet Beam: 57 feet Draught: 27 feet
Machinery	Triple expansion of 2,500 ihp to one shaft
Speed	11 knots

Notes: the official description of *Fort Langley* was Merchant Fleet Auxiliary.

The RFA's *Fort Rosalie* and *Fort Sandusky* with the MFA *Fort Langley* were used as armament stores carriers. *Fort Charlotte* was a stores issuing ship.

41st Royal Marine Independent Commando

The 41st Royal Marine Independent Commando were sent to Japan early in the Korean War. It was anticipated that there would be many suitable targets for raiding parties behind the front line, but the front line was so broken in the first four months of the War that it was very difficult to know exactly where the enemy was at times. During the Inchon landing they made a diversionary raid at Kunsan from HMS *Whitesand Bay*, with American Special Forces, but perhaps one of their most difficult tasks was when they fought their way from Hamhung to join the American Marine Division at Hagaru during the first Chinese offensive in April 1951. The Royal Marine Commandos fought with US troops through the mountain passes with the Communists close on each side of the road. With the aid of tanks of the 7th US Marines, the convoy, which comprised reinforcements for the US Army, the US Marines and the Commandos managed to force its way through.

On 7 April, 1951 250 RMC went ashore 8 miles south of Songjin and demolished part of the coastal railway, blowing up hundreds of yards of track with a crater sixteen feet deep. Bombardment was supplied from the USS *St Paul* with a fire control party with the RMC on shore.

RMC detachments from HMS *Ceylon* and *Kenya* made demonstration landings on the west coast opposite Cho-do Island, after ROKN minesweepers had swept the inshore waters. The RMC landed shore parties on several islands in the Bay of Wonsan on 28/29 September 1951, a further raid was made in the vicinity of Chaho with gun fire support from HMS *Belfast*, with a further raid north on 4/5 October. *Belfast* was supporting the RMC from 26/30 September visiting Wonsan, Songjin and Chongjin and carrying out bombardments at each. Her support of the RMC at Chaho enabled her to claim the furthest north bombardment on both coasts in one month. The Battle of the Islands also included members of the RMC, with US Marines and ROK Marines, plus RN personnel patrolling in small boats keeping contact with the islands and investigating junks.

On the east coast raids were carried out on the nights of 4/5 December by two troops from the islands of Yo-do and Mo-do. The parties landed from the USS *Horace A. Bass*, damaging railway tunnels and inflicting casualties. On 23 December, after a successful raid against enemy sampans in Wonsan Bay, the RMC were withdrawn to return to the UK.

HMAS Sydney entering harbour with her ship's company manning the side, and aft of the island a flight deck of aircraft. Courtesy Australian War Memorial.

Majestic Class Light Fleet Carrier HMAS *Sydney*

———

HMAS	COMMENCED	COMPLETED	BUILDER
Sydney (ex *Terrible*)	1943	1949	HM Dockyard (Devonport)

Displacement	14,380 tons Full load 19,550 tons
Armament – gun	4 × 3 pdr saluting guns
	30 × 40 mm on single and twin mountings
Aircraft	Fixed and folding wing – up to 40
Dimensions	Length: 698 feet Beam: 90 feet Draught: 25 feet
Flight deck	Length: 690¾ feet Width: 112½ feet
	Arrester wires 6 no Catapult 1 no
Hangar	Length: 445 feet Width: 52 feet
	Lifts 2 no
Machinery	Single reduction geared turbines to 2 shafts giving 42,000 shp
Speed	24¾ knots
Range	10,000 nm at 14 knots

Fuel	Ship: 3,000 tons
	Aircraft: 34,000 Imperial gallons
Complement	1350

HMAS	IN THEATRE	TO	MILES STEAMED
Sydney	September, 1951	January, 1952	40,000

Korean Service

HMAS *Sydney* arrived in theatre to relieve HMS *Glory* who proceeded to Australia for refit. She joined the WCSG off the west coast on 4 October but on the 8th steamed to the east coast to commence CAS against the enemy troop concentrations and ammunition dumps and similar targets. She also flew CAP for the USS *New Jersey* which was bombarding the same coastline.

On 14th October *Sydney* had to ride out typhoon Ruth, suffering damage to all the ship's boats, and six of the thirteen aircraft on the flight deck being write-offs.

By the 18th she had returned to the west coast striking at NK troop-carrying junks threatening the UN-held island of Taehwa-do and providing CAP to the 1st Commonwealth Division hitting bridges, roads, etc. On the 23rd she searched for ditched US pilots, some of whom were picked up by HMAS *Murchison*. Two days later she had two aircraft down and one damaged but no casualties. One pilot was rescued from a mudflat by *Amethyst*.

She continued with airstrikes and CAP against the railway tunnel between Haeju and Chaeryong. A Firefly was shot down behind enemy lines but with cover from the CAP and the Royal Australian Air Force Meteor jets in the area, the USN helicopter loaned to *Sydney* reached the aircrew just before the enemy and returned safely to the carrier.

Sydney was relieved by the USS *Rendova* and arrived in Kure on 28 October. She was back in theatre by 5 November with HMCSs *Athabaskan*, *Cayuga*, *Sioux* and the USSs *Hanna* and *Collett*, and continued with the usual airstrikes with one pilot fatality on 5 November. By the 12th she had flown her 1,000th sortie and had been striking the batteries at Hungnam in conjunction with *Belfast* off the east coast and she sailed for Sasebo on the 13th having been joined earlier by the USS *New Jersey*.

Having taken on the necessary stores she sailed from Sasebo on the 18th to the east coast striking Hungnam but returned to the west coast on the 22nd. The weather had been bad for a few days improving on the 27th with four days flying cancelled. Air strikes were flown but on the 7 December she had a pilot fatality whose aircraft had been hit by flak over Chinnampo with four further aircraft damaged. She continued her CAS until 17 December then steamed for Kure. She had been attacking NK troops near Changyon and Hanchon, batteries and similar targets at Chinnampo but lost an aircraft over Ongjin with the aircrew rescued by a US helicopter from Paengynong-do the following day. She also flew CAP over Cho-do-Sok-do and elsewhere. On 27 December she sailed and relieved the USS *Baedong Strait* proceeding to the west coast with *Tobruk* and on 1 January 1952 she was again striking at the enemy with CAP for UN troops at Yongyu-do and CAS as the island had been invaded by enemy troops. Bad weather prevailed on 17 January but her aircraft continued to operate until 25th her last operational day in theatre when with *Tobruk* she sailed for Sasebo and home. *Sydney* had 64 days in theatre with no flying on 12 days due to bad weather averaging 55 sorties per day. Expended were 1,402 bombs of up to 1,000 lb weight, 6,359 rocket projectiles and 269,249 rounds of 20 mm cannon.

HMAS Bataan. Courtesy Australian War Memorial.

HMAS Warramunga. Courtesy Australian War Memorial.

Australian Tribal Class Destroyers

HMAS	COMMENCED	COMPLETED	BUILDER
Bataan (ex *Kurnai*)	1942	1945	Cockatoo Docks & Eng. Co.
Warramunga	1940	1942	Cockatoo Docks & Eng. Co.

Displacement	1,927 tons Full load 2,745 tons
Dimensions	Length: 355¼ feet Beam: 36½ feet Draught: 9 feet
Armament – gun	6 (3 twin) LA 4.7" at A, B and Y positions
	2 (twin) 4"DP/AA at X position
	8 × 40 mm AA on single and twin mountings
Torpedo Tubes	4 (1 quad) 21"
Machinery	Geared turbines of 44,000 shp to 2 shafts
Speed	34 knots
Complement	290

HMAS	IN THEATRE	TO	MILES STEAMED
Bataan	June 1950	June 1951	57,000
	January 1952	September 1952	41,000
Warramunga	August 1950	August 1951	68,000
	January 1952	August 1952	44,000

Korean Service

HMAS *Bataan* with *Shoalhaven* was visiting Hong Kong at the commencement of the Korean War sailing for Okinawa and arriving there on 1 July and deployed to convoy escort duties in the Strait of Korea. On 13 July she took part in the US-inspired landing at Pohang to harass the advancing NK troops but this affair was not a success. She had been employed as a gunfire support ship with the USSs *Kyes*, *Higbee* and *Collett*. However on the 21st she sailed for Haeju-man to join the WCSG. She joined the carrier screen, returning to Pusan in late August and on 1 September was patrolling off the west coast blockading the approaches to Kunsan and Inchon after dark. From 4/6 September she was again screening *Triumph* which spotted for *Jamaica* during her bombardments of targets in the Kunsan and Inchon areas and again on the 7th. *Bataan* returned to Sasebo on the 11th returning to sea the following day screening *Triumph* again with HMAS *Warramunga* recently arrived in theatre.

SIC *Charity*, *Cockade* and *Concord* all gathered together for the Inchon landing on 15 September remaining in that area for some days. On the 27th *Bataan* with *Athabaskan* blockaded the Kunsan approaches with bombardment day and night of Osik-do newly reinforced by NK troops. The two destroyers were also on the lookout for drifting mines and destroyed four, and bombarded Beija Bay prior to being relieved by *Warramunga* on the 29th. *Bataan* returned to Sasebo on 4 October for R&R, boiler clean, etc. in anticipation of the Wonsan landing. Ten days later she was back at sea off the west coast screening HMS *Theseus* until 7 November when she escorted a US dredger to Chinnampo. *Bataan* returned to the west coast on the 14th and joined *Ceylon* until the 22nd, she had had a quiet time part being anchored off Taechong-do. On 4 December *Bataan* was in the force overseeing the evacuation of Chinnampo which entailed transit of a moored minefield, shallows and a narrow channel to evacuate casualties and other personnel and provide flak and gunfire support. The evacuation was completed quite late on the 5th with suitable targets desirable to the enemy being bombarded and set on fire. From 7/17 *Bataan* was again screening *Theseus* and supporting the UN ground forces and in January was repeating her performance at Chinnampo, this time at Inchon, until the 9th when she sailed for Kure for drydocking.

On 21 February HMAS *Bataan* was in company with the USS *Bataan* and the following day with *Belfast* commenced inshore patrols off Chinnampo and south to Inchon. The weather was severe for that period with ice-cold temperatures and strong winds and during 2/6 March an amphibious demonstration was made to the north of Haeju with the intentions of relieving the ground forces of the UN. Her duties at this time consisted of bombardment, escort, patrolling and all this in a temperature of 13°F. On 6 March she sailed for Sasebo but returned to sea on 13 March screening her namesake, USS *Bataan*, being relieved by the USS *Borie*. She continued on patrol in the Inchon approaches, until the 25th with two days in harbour, then proceeding to Sasebo. In April when screening her namesake, SIC were *Theseus*, *Consort*, *Athabaskan*, *Huron* and the USSs *English* and *Sperry*, on the east coast to strike the Wonsan area. The seas were rough with high speed steaming which necessitated a RAS four times in six days. Later that month she joined *Warramunga*, screening *Glory* with the USSs *Richard B. Anderson* and *Perkins*. By the 28th HMAS *Bataan* was again off the west coast screening *Glory* and the USS *Bataan*. This task concluded on 6 May, and on the 10th, she left Sasebo with *Huron* and *Glory* for the west coast, the weather was suitable for CAP and on the 18th she sailed to Kure, later proceeding to Hong Kong from which port on 29 May she sailed home to Australia, being relieved by HMAS *Murchison*.

On 4 February 1952 HMAS *Bataan* returned to theatre relieving *Murchison*, and continued on the west coast. Her first patrol was through the islands and on 10th February she did a RAS off Taechong-do with *Warramunga*, also in company were HMS *Charity* and *Mounts Bay*, with the usual routines patrolling in the Sokdo-Chodo area to the south of Chinnampo. On the 13th, with CAP from *Glory* she bombarded an enemy troop concentration near the village of Pungchon. That day the batteries were active and one hit was received on the captain's day cabin, with 78 rounds fired in return which created a conflagration at the enemy battery positions, and on the 24th she bombarded across the coastline inland below Chodo, finally withdrawing and proceeding to Sasebo. She returned to the west coast on 7 March screening the USS *Bairoko* with *Cayuga* and *Concord*, proceeding inshore after dark and bombarding between Sunwi-do and Changsan-jot Pt. Between 23/31st she was in company with *Cayuga* and the USS *Isbell*, at this time the carrier was HMS *Glory*. The patrol ceased in atrocious weather which did not permit flying and she sailed to Sasebo on 22 March. During April she was back screening the carrier on the west coast until the 10th, then joined *Belfast* in the task of defending the UN-held islands near the Haeju estuary, with responsibility for raiding parties of the RMC and USMC.

The island deemed essential to the UN cause was Taeyonpyong-do, with other craft in the vicinity to support, such as LCVPs, LSTs, minesweepers and patrol craft. 13th April brought an attempt to invade by NK troops crossing the mudflats, which required a creeping barrage from *Bataan* between Yongmae-do in Haeju Bay. On 20 April *Bataan* was relieved by *Whitesand Bay* off Haeju-man.

The following month was largely uneventful, screening and patrolling and defending the islands in the Haeju-man, Chodo and Sokdo areas, and in May *Bataan* was relieved by *Rotoiti*. In June *Bataan* was screening HMS *Ocean* and later steamed to the east coast bombarding Chongjin and similar targets and on the 21st she arrived in Kure for refit. By 21 July *Bataan* was again screening her namesake with VA John Collins the Australian Chief of Naval Staff on board. In company with *Newcastle*, she visited Paengnyong-do returning to Inchon to disembark her senior officer, then proceeded to Kure.

17 August brought her final patrol proceeding to the Haeju-man area and relieving *Concord*, with the USS *Strong* in company. The enemy batteries were quite active and she made a suitable reply. 30 August 1952 was her last operational day, and the following day she left theatre.

HMAS *Warramunga* entered theatre in August 1950 via Hong Kong arriving on the 25th escorting *Ceylon* and *Unicorn* who were on this occasion acting as troop carriers for two battalions of British troops, arriving at Pusan on the 28th. *Warramunga* had little time to acclimatize and soon joined the WCSG, the blockade routines were soon to become familiar. On 3 September she was in the screen with *Triumph* off the west coast with *Charity*, *Cockade* and *Concord* forming part of the assault group for the Inchon landing which occupied her for some days. At this time the UN became aware that many of the islanders on the west coast islands had been by-passed by the war and it fell to *Warramunga* to organise the emergency feeding of these people and of several lighthouse keepers and their families. She returned for more stores and delivered them to those who had been largely without food for three months. On 29 September she relieved *Bataan* and embarked FO2IC for an inspection tour, later she relieved *Athabaskan* for the Kunsan patrol and continued with patrols and bombardments until 4 October. On the 8th she arrived at Sasebo to join the units of the USN for the amphibious landing at Wonsan, which included the USSs *Missouri*, *Helena*, *Worcester* and HMS *Ceylon*. Her task was bombarding Chongjin, particularly the railway sidings and junctions. For the remainder of the month she was mine detecting and screening and as duty destroyer to the carriers, also acting as control ship at Wonsan. On the 31st she proceeded to the Yalu Gulf through rough seas and bad weather. The evacuation from Chinnampo has already been described under the account for HMAS *Bataan*, but *Warramunga* played her part in that event, the operation concluding on 5 December, the remainder of the month was patrolling the west coast and screening HMS *Theseus*, spending Christmas Day in harbour at Inchon.

By January 1951 the retreat from the north was still in progress and *Warramunga* assisted in the evacuation of UN troops with *Bataan*, *Ceylon* and the USS *Rochester*. On 3 February she was off the east coast bombarding Kangnung with the USS *English* and later screening the USSs *Manchester* and *Missouri*. With the USS *Lind* she steamed north to where the latter had previously landed agents, both ships bombarding after dark, with a later report stating that members of the NK Intelligence and police had been killed and wounded. Continuing north the destroyers maintained their bombardments prior to making course for Sasebo. Later in February the two destroyers with *Belfast* bombarded Wonsan, making their approach through minefields, then anchoring offshore with air strikes and support, which forced the coastal road to be abandoned for that period, which concluded with *Warramunga* being relieved by the USS *Borie* on 4 March. She experienced hull damage with some damage to her superstructure due to severe weather and gales, lying in port until early April, for repairs.

On 11 April she relieved *Black Swan* off the west coast and later moved to supervise a patrol of ROKN vessels gaining intelligence for *Belfast* in the Yalu Gulf. She then proceeded to Haeju-man to supervise ROKN minesweepers for two days, then joined *Comus* with whom she bombarded Inchon. By 26 April she was screening *Glory* with *Bataan* and the USSs *Richard B. Anderson* and *Perkins*, proceeding out of theatre on 4 May. *Warramunga* during the latter part of May and 1 June was on the west coast with the USS *Bataan*, where she remained until the 12th in company of the USS *Sicily*. Following this task she took part in the Han river demonstration screening *Glory* and USS *Sicily* with *Huron* and *Cayuga* and the USSs *Moore* and *Renshaw*. During the screen *Renshaw* made an Asdic contact which appeared to be a submarine, she was joined by *Moore* and both using up their A/S munitions; *Warramunga* continued the attack with her Squid but it turned out to be non-sub. On 29 July she returned to Sasebo and on 1 August joining *Ceylon* at Haeju-man bombarding from very close inshore, with CAP from USS *Sicily*. On 7 August she engaged the enemy batteries with 110 rounds bringing 12 months service in theatre to a close, and on the 24 August was relieved by HMAS *Anzac* at Sasebo.

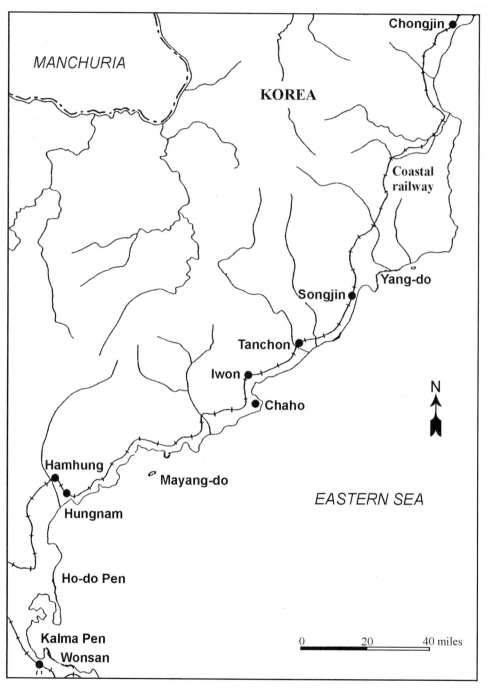

MANCHURIA

KOREA

Chongjin ●

Coastal
railway

Yang-do

Songjin ●

Tanchon ●

Iwon ●

● Chaho

N

Hamhung ●

Mayang-do

EASTERN SEA

Hungnam ●

Ho-do Pen

Kalma Pen

Wonsan ●

| 0 | 20 | 40 miles |

WONSAN TO CHONGIN. REDRAWN FROM *HISTORY OF UN FORCES IN THE
KOREAN WAR (II)*, COURTESY MINISTRY OF NATIONAL DEFENCE, REPUBLIC OF KOREA.

In February 1952 HMAS *Warramunga* returned to theatre and on the 7th joined the nightly patrol off Paengnyong-do. The following day it was learned that Mahap-do had been taken during the night, she bombarded the enemy and the same day joined the screen with *Glory*, detaching on 16 February for Kure for ten days refit. She sailed on the 25th to the east coast to relieve HMNZS *Taupo* off Songjin, bombarding the latter, the coastal railway and Yang-do with the USS *Doyle*. She continued bombarding in March off Yang-do and on the 2nd north of Chongjin was straddled by a salvo from five enemy guns of which she silenced three, and was relieved by *Morecambe Bay*, then steaming for Wonsan which she reached on the 8th. She continued screening *Glory* with improved weather, which turned so bad in strong gales that the carrier and her screen returned to Sasebo on the 22nd. The following month, April brought another ten days with *Glory*, then a trip to Hong Kong for repairs to her gun mountings, not returning until the beginning of May, off Chodo, relieving HMNS *Piet Hein*, in company with HMS *Crane*.

On passage to Wonsan *Warramunga* bombarded three batteries and she was joined by *Amethyst* for the usual routines but on the 17th she relieved the USS *Thomas* near Chongjin and covered the minesweepers, at the same time bombarding up to Songjin and expending 222 rounds of 4.7". She continued bombarding the coastal railway and covering the minesweepers, being joined the following day by the USS *Iowa*. *Warramunga* was off Chongjin on the 27th still bombarding the coastal railway, being relieved the following day by HMCS *Nootka*. In June she was off the west coast screening the USS *Bataan* and defending Chodo and Sokdo up to the 29th with the usual blockade routines. Finally on 12 July once again she was screening the USS *Bataan* but by 26 July she was at Kure and that day sailed home to Australia.

HMAS Anzac preparing to RAS. Courtesy Australian War Memorial.

HMAS Tobruk. Courtesy Australian War Memorial.

Australian Battle Class Destroyers

HMAS	COMMENCED	COMPLETED	BUILDERS
Anzac	1946	1951	Williamstown Naval Dockyard
Tobruk	1946	1950	Cockatoo Docks & Engineering Co. Pty

Displacement	*Anzac* 2,440 tons 3,450 tons full load
	Tobruk 2,436 tons
Dimensions	Length: 379 feet Beam: 41 feet Draught: 13½ feet (mean)
Armament – gun	4 (2 twin) DP/AA 4.5" in turrets at A and B positions.
	12 × 40 mm AA on single and twin mountings
Torpedo Tubes	10 (2 quin) 21"
Machinery	Geared turbines of 50,000 shp to 2 shafts
Speed	35¾ (designed); 31 knots (sea speed)
Complement	290

HMAS	IN THEATRE	TO	MILES STEAMED
Anzac	August 1951	October 1951	22,000
	September 1952	June 1953	30,000
Tobruk	September 1951	February 1952	39,000
	May 1953	October 1953	17,500

Korean Service

HMAS *Anzac* arrived at Sasebo on 24 August, 1951 as the replacement for HMAS *Warramunga*. She sailed from Sasebo for the west coast and joined the WCSG commencing the blockade routine which would soon become so familiar. On 6 September, she was bombarding off Haeju-man at pre-selected targets and returned to Sasebo that day. For the remainder of September she was deployed off the east coast blockading and bombarding off Wonsan and Songjin. By 26 September she had fired over 1000 rounds of 4.5" ammunition and sailed for Kure departing on 30 September escorting HMS *Glory* for R&R and refit in Australia.

HMAS *Anzac* at the commencement of her second tour arrived at Sasebo on 27 September 1952 and rejoined the WCSG on coastal patrol with *Newcastle* and *Rotoiti* off Paengnyong-do. For a week she was inshore and bombarding in the estuary of the Yalu river and off the Cholsan peninsula, then joined the carrier screen of HMS

Ocean relieving HMNS *Piet Hein*. From the screen she proceeded to Sasebo and Kure. In late October she returned to the west coast relieving *Nootka* and was tasked with the defence of Chodo and Sokdo with *Crusader* and *Comus*, also present were LSTs of the ROKN with CAP from *Ocean*. By 27 November she was back off the west coast with *Piet Hein* and the USS *Hickox*, the three screening *Glory*, but on 7 December *Anzac* relieved *Crusader* and carried on with bombarding and patrolling off Chodo and Sokdo being herself relieved on the 12th by *Comus* and *Anzac* returned to Sasebo the following day.

Her next patrol was off the east coast commencing 19 December where she relieved HMCS *Haida* defending Yang-do. She spent both Christmas and New Year at sea but was relieved arriving in Kure on 5 January, 1953. Her next task commenced on 21 January, 1953 again guarding Chodo and Sokdo with RFA *Wave Prince*, being relieved four days later by *Birmingham*. She continued with bombardments and gunfire support under dull skies and snow in temperatures of 9°F, continuing until Australia Day and on that day bombarding batteries she had first engaged the previous November. She was back in Sasebo on the 29th for R&R and maintenance, sailing on 5 February to join the screen for *Glory* off the west coast for some weeks with two breaks respectively at Kure and Sasebo. In April she was in company with *Culgoa* off Paengnyong-do and the USSs *Gurke* and *Maddox* based at Yangdo patrolling and bombarding the coastal railway. The following month she sailed for Tokyo where on 2nd June with HMS *Mounts Bay* she celebrated the Coronation of HM Queen Elizabeth II, representing the Commonwealth Naval Force.

In early June, *Anzac* with *Ocean* commenced her final patrol being relieved on 13 June by HMAS *Tobruk*, and arriving home by 3 July, 1953.

HMAS *Tobruk* was in theatre for September, 1951 having relieved *Anzac*, commencing operational duties on 3 October by screening the USS *Rendova*, returning to Sasebo on the 18th then sailing again on the same task from 26 October to 4 November. On the 8th she proceeded to the east coast blockading and bombarding enemy targets between Chongjin and Songjin including the coastal railway including the destruction of a goods train which became derailed, was then a sitting target and the 4.5" guns did the rest. She expended quite a quantity of ammunition as usual needing RAS then had a two-day excursion to Hungnam with HMAS *Sydney*, *Belfast*, *Van Galen* with bombardment and air strikes hitting the city. She then sailed to Kure for one week but was again at sea by 28 November again screening the USS *Rendova* until 6 December but the following day was screening *Sydney* off the west coast near Changyon, Hanchon and Chinnampo. On the 17th *Tobruk* joined *Ceylon*, *Constance* and the USSs *Manchester* and *Eversole* bombarding south of Sok-do, returning to Kure on 20 December. On New Year's Day 1952 *Tobruk* was at sea off Haeju and relieved *Whitesand Bay* bombarding as required with specific retaliation against the enemy attempting to capture Yongmae-do from Chomi-do, being relieved by *Cayuga* on the 9th.

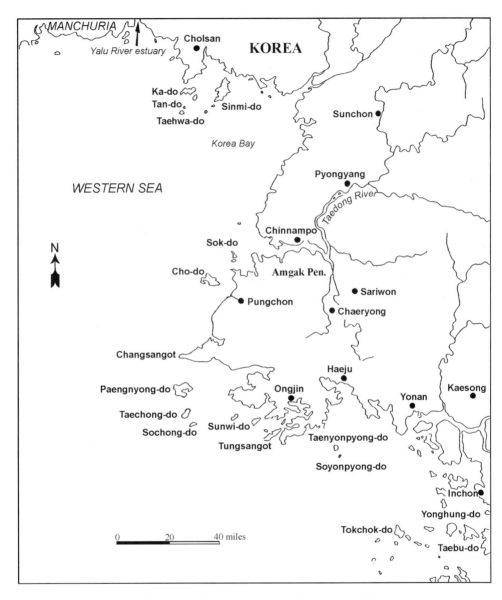

YALU RIVER TO TAEBU-DO. REDRAWN FROM *HISTORY OF UN FORCES IN THE KOREAN WAR (II)*, COURTESY MINISTRY OF NATIONAL DEFENCE, REPUBLIC OF KOREA.

By the 16th she was again screening *Sydney* with *Sioux* and the USSs *Hanson* and *Radford* until the 25th when she was off Chodo and Sokdo bombarding during daylight hours and guarding the islands after dark. The following day, *Tobruk* sailed via Sasebo for home.

In May 1953 HMAS *Tobruk* returned to theatre and commenced the bombardments and inshore patrols the following month relieving *Anzac* on 13 June 1953 and on 26 June with *Newcastle* was off the west coast near Taechong-do. The following day she was deployed to screen HMS *Ocean* until 5 July when the USS *Bairoko* relieved *Ocean*.

Later in the month *Tobruk* was off the east coast to relieve *Huron* joining the Yangdo blockade and engaged in patrolling which resulted in her gunnery being used to sink a suspected mine-laying sampan on the 16th. She continued with her patrol and engaged an enemy radar station at Musudan Pt on the 24th east-nor-east of Yangdo with effective results from her 4.5" main armament, these were her final shots of the Korean War.

HMAS Condamine. Courtesy Australian War Memorial

HMAS Culgoa. Courtesy Australian War Memorial.

HMAS Murchison. Courtesy Australian War Memorial.

HMAS Shoalhaven. Courtesy Australian War Memorial.

Australian Bay Class Frigates

————

HMAS	COMMENCED	COMPLETED	BUILDER
Condamine	1943	1945	New South Wales Government Engineering & Shipbuilding, Newcastle
Culgoa (ex *MacQuarie*)	1942	1944	Williamstown Naval Dockyard, Melbourne
Murchison	1944	1946	Evans, Deakin & Co. Ltd.
Shoalhaven	1943	1945	Brisbane & Walker Ltd., Maryborough

Displacement	1,544 tons Full load 2,187 tons
Dimensions	Length: 301 feet Beam: 36½ feet Draught: 12 feet
Armament – gun	4 (2 twin) DP/AA 4" in B & X positions
	3 × 40 mm AA
	8 × 20 mm AA
Anti submarine	1 Hedgehog
	4 × depth charge throwers
Machinery	Triple expansion 5,500 ihp to 2 shafts
Speed	19 knots
Fuel	500 tons oil fuel
Range	5180 nm at 12 knots
Complement	177

HMAS	IN THEATRE	TO	MILES STEAMED
Condamine	July, 1952	April, 1953	31,000
Culgoa	April, 1953	October, 1953	16,000
Murchison	May, 1951	February, 1952	36,000
Shoalhaven	June ,1950	September, 1950	11,000

Korean Service

Condamine commenced her operational duties on patrol off Haeju-man on 4 August having arrived in theatre the previous month. She relieved the USS *Kimberly* on the 8th off the Taedong river engaging the Amgak batteries but after dark cruising between Chodo and the mainland guarding against infiltration parties. A week later she was bombarding in conjunction with the air strikes providing no let up for the enemy gunners.

After spending 16th in typhoon Karen, *Condamine* was relieved by *St Brides Bay*, entering Sasebo on the 19th. Three days later she sailed for the east coast off Songjin, her task was the defence of Yangdo and bombarding the coastal railway between Chaho and Chongjin. In this she had some success, hitting a goods train with two locomotives which split into two self-propelled halves with evident damage but still mobile and seeking shelter from her gunfire in cuttings and a tunnel. On the 10th she demolished six munition stores at Tanchon and was relieved by HMS *Charity* the following day, proceeding to Kure for ten days. She returned to sea on 22 September and relieved *St Brides Bay* on the 23rd off Haeju-man working with units of the ROKN in defence of the offshore islands for two weeks with night stations to the east of Taesuap-do and during the day off Taeyonpyong-do. The 23rd brought a raid by UN Special Forces against Chomi-do which she supported but the raiders withdrew leaving *Condamine* with two US wounded. From 7 October she was patrolling off the Chodo Sokdo area with little action. In the middle of the month she was subjected to bad weather off Paengnyong-do maintaining the island watch as before but with some daily bombardment. She provided close support for the minesweeping activities off Sokdo for two days, then patrolled off Haeju-man until 8 November. The ten day patrols off Haeju-man and Paengnyong-do alternating with seven day visits to Kure continued until 6 January 1953.

Condamine returned to patrolling and bombarding from 21 January until 15 March off Chodo and Haeju-man. She was relieved by HMAS *Culgoa* who arrived at Sasebo on 14 April permitting *Condamine* to leave theatre and steam for home.

HMAS *Culgoa* relieved *Condamine* and commenced her first patrol by relieving *Whitesand Bay* on 19 April off Paengnyong-do, anchoring in daylight hours but cruising after dark maintaining patrol security and bombarding as required, this routine she kept until 28 April when she was relieved by HMNZS *Kaniere*. Earlier she had supported partisans allied to the UN on the mainland firing 102 rounds of 4" to good effect silencing mortars. She bombarded again on the 26th but the enemy could not to be found, proceeding on the 28th to the Chodo Sokdo area where she supported *Haida* until 3 May then retiring. She was back at sea on 18 May off Chodo and bombarding the Amgak batteries for five days then on the 20th assisting the USS *Cocopa* in salvaging an RN aircraft south of Chodo. *Culgoa* relieved HMS *Sparrow* off Taeyonpyong-do having been herself relieved on the 23rd by *St Brides Bay*. She found herself in charge of 11 ROKN vessels (including 2 minesweepers and 3 patrol craft) escorting over 700 junks engaged in fishing, a task which she found uneventful, sailing for Kure on 7 June.

Later in the month back at sea she was patrolling off the west coast near Haeju-man guarding Taeyonpyong-do and on the 13th coordinating her bombardment with air strikes against Yongmae-do by the USS *Bairoko* as that island had been invaded by NK troops. HMAS *Culgoa* was relieved by HMS *Charity* on 19 June and proceeded out of theatre to Hong Kong.

HMAS *Murchison* had relieved HMAS *Bataan* in May, 1951 and commenced patrolling off the west coast in June which proved to be a quiet period.

In July she was bombarding off the Yalu river and the Chinnampo approaches south of Chodo Island and the Taedong estuary with enemy armour and soft vehicles as targets. Later in July *Murchison* with *Cardigan Bay* and ROKN PF52 entered the estuary of the Han to demonstrate UN influence in that area. They were reinforced by *Morecambe Bay* and 6 other ROKN vessels to carry out regular bombardment of suitable targets including troop concentrations. The ship's boats were occupied for some days with hydrographic surveys of the many channels.

After escort duties off Inchon she steamed back to the Han on 10 August to join *Cardigan Bay* and ROKN PF 52. She continued to bombard and gather hydrographic information until late August, then a period of R&R and maintenance before returning to the Han for the established estuary routine. Neap tides meant less water but better ability to see the mudflats. She was shell splashed and saw a ROKN hydrographic ML hit by an enemy shell. On 28 September *Murchison* embarked RA G. Dyer, USN making an inspection of his area of command. This brought fire from the shore as mortars, 50 mm and 75 mm pieces fired at the frigate which replied in kind while steaming in a narrowing channel in which she altered course 180° by steaming round her anchor. The batteries she engaged were silenced but she sustained four hits with minimal damage and slight injury to one rating. Two days later she returned and had a further close range engagement hitting the offending batteries and in this incident expending 276 rounds of 4" and lesser calibre ammunition. At this time *Black Swan* was in company and CAS from the USS *Rendova*. On 1 October *Murchison* that day sailed for drydock at Kure.

On the 17th she was back at sea escorting the RFA *Wave Prince*, then to Inchon on patrol for four days and on the 21st with *Hawea* cruising off the Yalu Gulf then patrolling off Chinnampo. In November it was back to the Han to relieve *St Brides Bay* off Sok-do and bombarding the Amgak batteries until the 5th. She continued an offensive patrol in the Han estuary, bombarding and using information from Special Forces to select her targets until 16 November when she was relieved by *Whitesand Bay* and headed for R&R at Kure.

HMAS *Murchison* arrived at Paengnyong-do on 27 November, patrolling off Taehwa-do until the month's end then to Chodo and Bokdo area. On 3 December she proceeded to Inchon to join the carrier screen, from thence she steamed to Sasebo to RAS then onward to Hong Kong for R&R and maintenance. At the New Year she was back in Sasebo and on 22 January, 1952 was again off the west coast in the Han estuary bombarding batteries and likely targets. On the 28th she steamed to Taechong-do protecting as far as possible the island of Yuk-som for two days which proved to be rather quiet, then returned to the Han and bombardments based on intelligence, expending 150 rounds of 4" ammunition. As her gunnery came to an end she altered course for Sasebo, thus concluding her service in the Korean War.

HMAS *Shoalhaven* on 21 June 1950 was at Hong Kong on a routine visit and on 1 July sailed for Okinawa. Her first task was as escort to a US troop transport with the US Fleet Tug *Arikari* from Sasebo to Pusan. She was then deployed to the west coast relieving the USS *De Haven* on the 7th and having the USS *Collett* in company for three days then she returned to Sasebo. She remained in theatre on various tasks including Sasebo-Pusan convoys until 6 September when she sailed home to Australia.

HMCS Athabaskan. Courtesy Public Archives Canada.

HMCS Cayuga. Courtesy Public Archives Canada.

HMCS Haida. Courtesy Public Archives Canada.

HMCS Huron. Courtesy Public Archives Canada.

HMCS Iroquois in Korean waters. Courtesy Maritime Command Museum Halifax.

HMCS Nootka. Courtesy Public Archives Canada.

Canadian Tribal Class Destroyers

―――――

HMCS	COMMENCED	COMPLETED	BUILDER
Athabaskan	1944	1918	Halifax Shipyards Ltd.
Cayuga	1943	1947	Halifax Shipyards Ltd.
Haida	1941	1943	Vickers Armstrong (Tyne)
Huron	1941	1943	Vickers Armstrong (Tyne)
Iroquois	1940	1942	Vickers Armstrong (Tyne)
Nootka	1942	1946	Halifax Shipyards Ltd.

Displacement	1,927 tons Full load 2,745 tons
Dimensions	Length: 355 feet Beam: 37½ feet Draught: 9½ feet (mean)
Armament – gun	

Athabaskan, Cayuga	*Haida*
8 (4 twin) 4" DP AA	6 (3 twin) 4.7" LA
6 × 40 mm AA	4 × 40 mm AA
4 × 20 mm AA	4 × 2 pdr AA
4 × 2 pdr AA	4 × 20 mm AA

Huron	*Iroquois*
6 (4 twin) 4" DP AA	6 (3 twin) 4.7" LA
4 × 40 mm AA	2 (twin) 4" DP AA
4 × 2 pdr AA	4 × 40 mm AA
2 × 20 mm AA	4 × 2 pdr AA
	2 × 20 mm AA

Nootka
8 (4 twin) 4" DP AA
4 × 40 mm AA
4 × 20 mm AA   Light weapons on single, twin or quad mtgs

Torpedo Tubes	4 (quad) 21"
Anti submarine.	1 Squid, except *Nootka*
Machinery	Geared turbines 44,000 shp to 2 shafts
Speed	34 knots
Fuel	520 tons oil fuel
Range	1,700 nm at 20 knots
Complement	240

HMCS	IN THEATRE	TO
Athabaskan	July 1950	September 1950
	May 1951	June 1952
	November 1952	November 1953
Cayuga	July 1950	March 1951
	July 1951	June 1952
	January 1954	November 1954
Haida	November 1952	June 1953
	February 1954	September 1954
Huron	March 1951	August 1951
	June 1953	February 1954
	October 1954	December 1954
Iroquois	June 1952	November 1952
	June 1953	January 1954
	August 1954	December 1954
Nootka	January 1951	July 1951
	February 1952	November 1952

Korean Service

HMCS *Athabaskan* arrived in theatre from Esquimalt via Pearl Harbour on 5 July, with *Cayuga* and *Sioux* arriving at Sasebo on 30 July 1950. The following day *Athabaskan* was escorting the USS *General Morton* (troopship) to Pusan and continued with the same task until the 11th when she joined the other Commonwealth ships off the west coast. She commenced to bombard the advancing enemy and related targets and supported ROK troops landing on NK-dominated islands. On 15 August following ROKN staff advice, she had arrived at Ochong-do and later engaged suspect junks and sampans. She bombarded a four-gun battery near Kunsan with 58 rounds of 4" with little reply, then moved to Taechon, bombarding an enemy OP with no response, and continued to patrol the closest islands.

The following day she was in company of ROKN YMS 502 and PC 704 holding a naval conference at which information was exchanged. She steamed south to Popsongpo which had been identified as a NK Field HQ which she shelled with good effect, then joined HMS *Kenya* off Inchon. There was good liaison between the CO of *Kenya* and the ROKN and it was agreed that *Athabaskan* would support that force the following day when a landing party from the two ROKN YMSs would take the island of Tokchok. Similarly on the 19th Yonghung-do was taken and a party from *Athabaskan* destroyed the radio at Palmi-do Lighthouse on the 20th. She continued to support ROKN activities but on 2 September was in Sasebo, sailing the following day for escort duties off the west coast. *Athabaskan* operated with ROKN PC 704 against Piung-do and Osik-do which were islands off Kunsan, and on 25 September she sent her cutters to reconnoitre Piung-do but found nothing of significance. The same day she was joined by YMS 306 which with PC 704 landed a party on Osik-do, but machine gun fire was received indicating resistance and little chance of overcoming the enemy at that time.

On the 21st *Athabaskan* investigated four mines sighted by PC 704 the previous day and destroyed one, dan buoyed another and plotted the positions of the remainder. A few days later she countermined the mines with charges at low water from one of her boats. The following day more mines were observed, and four were destroyed. Together with *Bataan*, she bombarded Osik-do then on the 28th bombarded targets at Beija Bay. After sunset *Athabaskan* steamed to the north noting enemy field works being prepared on Oejanggo-do which she engaged with her main armament. Enemy junks were absent from the scene and at daybreak she sailed for Inchon and embarked FO2IC for passage to Sasebo. On 10 October *Athabaskan* sailed for the east coast and Wonsan with *Cockade* and *Warramunga*, joining the US force with the three destroyers bombarding as usual. Later she screened the USS *Missouri*, *Helena*, *Worcester* and HMS *Ceylon*, then was detached to Tanchon with *Worcester* and *Ceylon* for bombardments, she also destroyed one mine. On 1 November she escorted *Missouri* to Sasebo.

Athabaskan was one of the units selected for support of the Chinnampo evacuation, which was completed by 7 December. From December until the New Year of 1951 the patrols continued, but *Athabaskan* required dockyard attention and on 22 December was at Sasebo for some time. By April, 1951 *Athabaskan* with *Huron* was screening *Theseus* and the USS *Bataan* off the east coast near Wonsan and later she was relieved by *Sioux* and sailed home to Canada on 3 May, 1951. She returned to theatre on 31 August and rejoined *Glory*'s carrier screen again off Wonsan during 18/19 September for bombardments and carrier strikes.

On 5 November *Athabaskan* relieved *Murchison* off Cho-do and commenced a bombardment of the Amgak batteries. The following day she went inshore towards Amgak just after sunrise shelling Kumbong-ni without any reply from the Amgak position. At the conclusion of her shoot she rejoined *Belfast* off Sok-do and took on a quantity of arms and ammunition with other stores for Taehwa-do which she delivered that evening, and shortly after Taehwa-do was under attack, strangely from the air. It was reported that eleven twin-engined bombers had appeared, this being the second enemy air raid on the island. Later she steamed north to the enemy-held Ka-do, with a list of targets which she bombarded during the night, clearing the area before sunrise. During the air raid at Taehwa-do there had been many casualties and it was the new task of *Athabaskan* to pick the wounded up and to land them at Inchon.

On 6th November *Athabaskan* was used as a decoy to draw fire from the batteries on the Amgak peninsula, hoping that they would reveal their positions to the waiting *Belfast* and a flight of *Sydney*'s Furies, but the enemy did not respond to the bait.

Just after midnight on the 9th, she was off Paengnyong-do but found that a US bomber had crashed, she lowered her cutter with her medical team and treated the survivors. 11/12th November was spent off Cho-do. During the 12/14th she was in the Yalu Gulf, but on the latter day was screening the carriers, entering Sasebo on the 23rd. Two days later she sailed to relieve *Cayuga,* reporting to *Ceylon* at Paengnyong-do on the 27th, She proceeded to the north-east of Sokdo with bad weather and a bad sea causing her to alter course to the lee of Chodo and to anchor. The next day she bombarded an OP on the Wolsari peninsula. She left Chodo to rejoin the carrier screen and on the 30th headed for Taehwa-do in company with HMS *Cockade* and on approaching Taehwa-do, it appeared to be a scene of chaos with many fires.

On 1 December shortly after setting an NK junk on fire, she returned again to Taehwa-do searching for survivors, she lowered her cutter which went to the shore but there was no response and it was obvious that Taehwa-do had fallen to the enemy. During the next two days *Athabaskan* along with other vessels assisted in the evacuation of non-combatants from Chodo before being relieved by *Van Galen* and leaving for Sasebo. During this period the Canadian destroyers were chiefly engaged on the defence of islands in the Yong Pyong-do and Chodo/ Sokdo areas, which continued over the next six months of 1952. During early January *Athabaskan* undertook one patrol off the east coast and was also screening *Sydney.* She was very active in bombarding the coastal railway, expending for this incident 1,292 rounds of 4" and 5,860 rounds of 40 mm ammunition.

From 20th to 24th January 1952 she was screening the USS *Baedong Strait* for air strikes in the Yellow Sea. At this period she was again defending Yuk-do and Wollae-do and continuing to bombard the mainland, refuelling at Taechong-do before returning to the screen. On the 29/30th she was again protecting the islands firing at any worthwhile target and at dusk patrolling off Yuk-do. The following four days were quiet but on 5 February she was still guarding Yuk-do but had to leave for Mahap-do. There were so many little islands so close to enemy territory that it was nearly impossible for the UN naval force to guard them against raids carried out after dark. The first eight days of March saw *Athabaskan* off Haeju-man being relieved by *Cossack* and sailing for Hong Kong for a period and R&R. During June she was again off the islands almost constantly in action off Mu-do, Yongmae-do and Kobuk-som. The night of 11/12th saw an attack on Yongmae-do with *Athabaskan* greatly assisted by *Ceylon,* she then moved to Sosuap-do with *Constance* not far away and ROKN PC 701 guarding Mu-do and AMC 301 guarding Yonpyong-do. She was also supporting a raid which was to take place north of Sosuap-do. She was relieved on 16 June by HMS *Amethyst* and proceeded to Sasebo en route for home.

In November 1952 *Athabaskan* was back in theatre for her third tour screening the USS *Baedong Strait* from 7 to 17th off Chodo and at the conclusion of the above she sailed to Kure to observe Christmas with *Crusader* and *Haida.* On New Year's Day, 1953 *Athabaskan* was off the west coast encountering ice floes and pack ice, and on the 18th when at anchor off Chodo she lost her anchor plus four shackles of cable, recovered four days later with the help of the USS Fleet tug *Quapaw.* During

February she was off the east coast bombarding the coastal railway and fortunately on the 18th sighted a US Navy jet aircraft crash into the sea just ahead of her, she soon had the pilot on board none the worse. The following day she relieved the USS *Thompson* and continued to bombard batteries and sank a mine on the 24th and was herself relieved by *Charity* on the 27th. March was quieter than normal with *Athabaskan* off Chodo until 1 April, and during this period she supported a number of raids on the mainland. May was again quiet with little to report apart from normal routine patrols.

However, in June she was again off the coastal railway when she bombarded three trains but did not completely destroy them due to low cloud and her inability to benefit from her star shell. The following night was better, which was also Dominion Day, by destroying a 24-coach train that she had halted with her main armament. During this period she relieved *Crusader* and joined the screen of the USS *Bairoko* with air strikes on the Wolsa-ri peninsula. In July *Athabaskan* was off the east coast and concentrated on railways but on the 7th was relieved by *Huron* and sailed for Sasebo. She returned to sea on the 18th off the Haeju-man area bombarding troop concentrations near Mu-do, and again screened the USS *Bairoko*. On 27 July came the cease-fire, but *Athabaskan* remained in theatre until 18 November, 1953.

HMCS *Cayuga* arrived at Sasebo with *Athabaskan* and *Sioux* on 30 July 1950. She was deployed to the west coast, being straightaway active in enforcing the blockade and on 3 August she escorted RFA *Brown Ranger* to RAS with other UN naval ships then carried out five convoy escort tasks to Pusan until the 24th. From that date she again deployed off the west coast. Earlier on the 15th, *Cayuga* with *Mounts Bay* and in between convoys, bombarded Yosu harbour as a foretaste of the tasks to come.

On the 31st, *Cayuga* with *Sioux* again bombarded, this time the target was on the island of Taebu-do consisting of enemy formations and dumps. Planning for the Inchon landing was a priority with *Cayuga* escorting ships of the logistic group. *Cayuga* relieved *Sioux* off Kunsan on 17 September, three days later she was relieved by *Athabaskan* but on the 22nd she bombarded Beijaa Bay again with *Athabaskan*. After a visit to Sasebo she returned to the west coast with *Sioux*, blockading north off Inchon and screening *Theseus*. On 19 October with *Kenya*, *Cayuga* narrowly missed entering a minefield which was fortunately detected by her Asdic operator. By 3 December she was off the Yalu with *Bataan* and *Athabaskan*. *Cayuga* headed for Chodo but took part in the Chinnampo operation which was concluded on the 6th. From that date she was frequently on patrol and only entered Sasebo on 8 January, 1951 for dry-docking.

On 25 January 1952 *Cayuga* with *Nootka* were leaving Inchon but the batteries at Wolmi-do engaged them; both destroyers reversed course, closed the batteries, silenced them and steamed even closer to let the 40 mm have a go at Wolmi-do which was good practice for the close range guns' crews. Two days later *Cayuga* returned to Inchon and on the 30th received further fire from the enemy batteries but with little result. HMCS *Cayuga* left Inchon on 3rd February, this time without any enemy response and continued with the routines. On 16 March *Cayuga* was relieved by *Huron* and sailed for home.

In July 1951 she had returned from Canada and was back in theatre off the west coast screening *Glory* and the USS *Sicily* for what turned out to be a quiet period at the height of summer off the Imjin, returning to Sasebo on 4 August. *Cayuga* patrolled off Chodo and Sokdo sailing on the 8th and bombarding OPs, batteries and NK troops. In company were the ROKN YMSs 511 and 512 which gave local intelligence, receiving fresh water and medical assistance from *Cayuga* which then anchored south of Sokdo and engaged targets she had learned about. Then she steamed to Cho-do and assisted local partisans for the next day or so, shielding friendly junks and bombarding Pungchon and numbers of the enemy on the mudflats, however she had to clear seaweed from her condensers that day. She bombarded close inshore, later anchoring for nightfall seaward of Sok-do. The next day, the 12th she was relieved by *Consort* and steamed to Inchon for a RAS with RFA *Wave Chief* then for the rest of the month from the 14th was screening the carrier off the west coast. This task continued into September when Wonsan was bombarded and suffered airstrikes on the 18/19.

Earlier in the month she had been inshore off Chodo relieving *Rotoiti* and finding targets to bombard. She again had the company of ROKN YMS 510 which she directed to minesweeping tasks, with *Belfast* also bombarding in the area. *Cayuga* visited Changsan-got and Hwanghae Province Promontory and bombarded yet again after dark using starshell for illumination. On 6 September she steamed to the Manchurian border at the Yalu river, investigating trade from Dairen to Antung. On the 7th she returned to Cho-do to assist with a raid at the Samchon beaches supporting guerillas, discharging 335 rounds of 4" in this action. There were seven friendly wounded who were treated and transferred to *Belfast*. *Cayuga* cruised north again to the Yalu but little occurred on this occasion and on the 13th she was relieved by *Sioux*.

During October she again screened *Sydney* and *Belfast* and bombarded Wonsan on the east coast returning to the west coast and Taechong-do. About the 22nd a B29 aircraft crash-landed on the island seen also by *Murchison*, both ships sent medical aid to find two aircrew in shock, but the others fine. On 25th Tae Wha-do was bombed by enemy single-engined aircraft, and *Cayuga* embarked several casualties and took them to Paengnyong-do. She proceeded to Sogaza-do and bombarded enemy batteries and military camps then to Sun-do for the same treatment and the following day *Ceylon* was in the area. On the 27th she was off the Taedong river then the next two days guarding Taehwa-do. On the 28th she was in the Chang San Got area bombarding close inshore hitting field artillery. Two days later, when sending a boat to the assistance of a friendly junk near Sok-to, she was fired on from the Amgak peninsula and had to slip her cable and make a rapid stern-board to get clear.

On 23/24 November *Cayuga* with *Hawea* and *Taupo* were off Cho-do and the following day bombarded batteries at Wolsa-ri, then sailed for Sasebo arriving on the 26th. By 1 December *Cayuga* was back off Cho-do being relieved by *Athabaskan* on the 7th for Sasebo, but was back at sea on the 20 December preparing for the Ung-do and Chongyang-do operation which were occupied by the enemy. She continued patrolling and island defence and on 1 January, 1952 proceeded to Taechong-do being relieved by *Van Galen*, she then set course for Taehwa-do to bombard then to Kure on the 4th. She was back at sea on the 8th off Haeju-man and relieved *Tobruk* at Yonpyong-do, the following night with ROKN PC 702 she bombarded Changnin-do destroying junks, sampans and a store of rice with enemy casualties. On the 11th she was at Taechong-do and bombarded Upchori village with its batteries. On the 14th January *Cockade* relieved *Cayuga* who proceeded to Sasebo thence to Hong Kong for refit and R&R. *Cayuga* returned to Cho-do for 6 to 16 April, then in the carrier screen off the west coast, then back to Cho-do 10 to 18 May bombarding as usual and on the 18th sailed for Kure and home.

HMCS *Haida* relieved *Nootka* on 12 November 1952 in Sasebo and was deployed to the west coast, screening the carrier *Glory* which proved to be uneventful and she returned to Sasebo on the 29th without engaging the enemy. On 3 December she was off the east coast and blockading from Yang-do to Chaho in range of the coastal railway which she finally engaged on the nights of 17/18th. The following day she was off Songjin in the early morning and a further train arrived and was stopped by her gunnery but when the smoke had cleared, the locomotive had disappeared. On the 20th she was relieved by *Anzac*. She spent Christmas with *Athabaskan* and *Crusader* at Kure, and had some time in the dockyard. In February 1953 she was back off the west coast on the inshore patrol bombarding batteries and troop concentrations near Mu-do. The following month saw her back off the east coast, train watching but with little effect as the railway appeared to be active only after dark, but in April she returned to screening the carrier.

On the 26th having returned from Hong Kong she was off Yang-do later Songjin concentrating on the coastal railway and preventing repairs being carried out. More than one train was sighted and her gunnery was good for the conditions, which were darkness, smoke and dust, near midnight a further train appeared but due to poor visibility escaped. She returned to Yang-do and patrolled northward with the USS *Bradford* and that night she engaged a northbound train with illumination by starshell but after the smoke had cleared once again the locomotive had disappeared into a tunnel. She continued to fire on the rolling stock then on the 30th for the balance of her time off the east coast, she sighted and sank a mine, gave gunfire support for USN minesweepers and bombardment of batteries to the north of Chongjin and Songjin. On 8 June, 1953 she was relieved by HMS *Cossack* and sailed for Sasebo, then home.

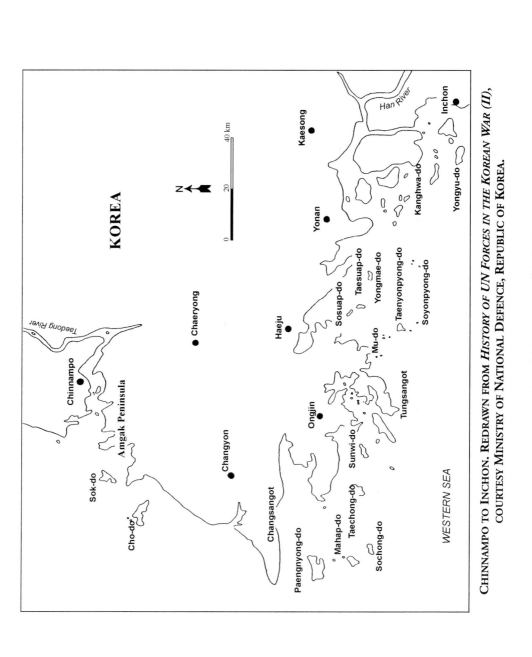

CHINNAMPO TO INCHON. REDRAWN FROM *HISTORY OF UN FORCES IN THE KOREAN WAR (II)*,
COURTESY MINISTRY OF NATIONAL DEFENCE, REPUBLIC OF KOREA.

HMCS *Huron* relieved *Cayuga* on 16 March, 1951 and after two or three weeks in the dockyard was patrolling off the west coast during April. She accompanied *Theseus* and the USS *Bataan* to attack Wonsan on the east coast with bombardments from the destroyers and airstrikes plus further bombardments from *Kenya* and at the conclusion of this operation she remained with the carrier screen and returned to the west coast. In May she became the first Commonwealth ship to capture a troop-carrying junk and bring it home with enemy POWs, on the same patrol she shelled a troop concentration of about 150 NK troops, then she assisted a Korean lighthouse keeper who was ill by giving medical aid.

A short time later, *Huron* did a RAS from RFA *Wave Premier* with *Glory* and during this RAS a rating from *Glory* fell into the sea and was picked up by *Huron*. July saw the commencement of operations in the Han which have been mentioned earlier with a similar operation south of latitude 38° near the Haeju estuary On 7 July she had been bombarding in the Songjin/Chongjin areas, but a gun positioned onshore by the southern end of the Songjin channel retaliated, but it was quickly silenced. On 11 August RA Scott-Moncrieff visited the Han and flew his flag from *Huron*. She then returned to Sasebo for a day then sailed to join the screen with *Glory*. On 14 August *Huron* sailed for home via Sasebo being relieved by *Athabaskan* who arrived in theatre about two weeks later.

HMCS *Iroquois* relieved *Cayuga* and on 23 June 1952 commenced an operational patrol off the west coast screening the USS *Bataan* for some days. She returned to Sasebo and after a period in the dockyard returned to sea in July. On the 28th she was off Paengnyong-do with HMNZS *Taupo,* when a number of enemy troop-carrying junks were observed which were then attacked by the frigates, but 90% of the action was completed by *Taupo* which was the closer. It was later learned that the junks had been attempting to invade Paengnyong-do but the action was sufficient to deter the enemy from trying this again. During August *Iroquois* was on the screen with the carriers and later in the month spent five days off the east coast with ships of the USN exercising through the war zone. In September she was on inshore patrol off Haeju-man and took part in a raid by Special Forces from Yongmae-do with *Belfast* and CAS from the USS *Sicily. Belfast* and *Iroquois* were bombarding with a fire control team onshore and at the close of the day the raid was deemed to be highly successful. On 14 September *Iroquois* was relieved by *St Brides Bay* and joined the screen with HMS *Ocean.* On the 28th she relieved *Charity* off the east coast. Four days later she bombarded Songjin but was hit by a retaliatory third shot which detonated by B gun, with one officer and one rating killed instantly. Four ratings were severely wounded and eight with injuries. She zig-zagged at full speed to get out of range and fortunately was not hit again. *Nootka* sent her medical team to assist but one of the seriously wounded later died, the dead being buried in the Commonwealth cemetery at Yokohama with full naval honours.

Iroquois remained with the task unit for a further 11 days but on 14 October was relieved by the USS *Carmick* and she then sailed for Sasebo. In the first two weeks of November she was at Hong Kong but sailed for the Haeju-man and Cho-do areas for the period 17 to 21st on the carrier screen. The following day she returned to Sasebo being relieved by *Athabaskan* and sailed home to Canada. She returned to theatre on 18 June 1953 and commenced the usual patrols, being from 22 to 27 June off Cho-do with bombardments. Then came the cease-fire, and *Iroquois* being the only Canadian destroyer to be involved, remained north of latitude 38° assisting in the evacuation of certain islands which had been allocated to the North Korean Government.

HMCS *Nootka* relieved *Sioux* on 12 February 1951 at Sasebo and after a settling down period she sailed for the Cho-do/Sok-do area but had some trouble with ice, and was then deployed to screen the carrier. During the latter days of March she proceeded to Haeju-man and returned to Cho-do in April. From May to 9 June she was off Yang-do, north-east of Songjin and relieved *Warramunga*, on 30 May she was engaged by enemy batteries below Chongjin, being straddled, but fortunately did not receive any hits. She was again straddled on 1 June as she cruised between Hungnam to Chongjin bombarding gun positions and the coastal railway, also junks, sampans and other likely targets. After sunset she moved inshore, continuing bombarding with starshell and during this period she fired 2,000 rounds of 4" ammunition. She was relieved by HMS *Constance* on 9 June and sailed for Hong Kong via Sasebo but on the 23rd returned to sea screening the USS *Bataan* off the west coast. During July she was again onshore near Haeju-man bombarding but with little return fire. The patrol continued until 4 August coming under fire seven times but without being hit. She had earlier taken part in a raid opposite Haeju port on 24 July, the details of this raid have been given earlier. She was relieved by *Concord* and returned to Kure for three weeks.

On 26 September *Nootka* whilst on radar watch had approached a junk which appeared to be laying mines. She launched her cutter which approached an object, which was a large inflated tube, with an NK officer inside about to open fire with a submachine gun, but he had been blinded by her searchlight. At daybreak, *Nootka* picked up a total of five that were in floating tubes, and they were treated according to the Geneva Convention. On 1 October she returned to *Ocean*'s carrier screen. In the first two weeks of October she had been with the carriers and *Iroquois*. Later off Cho-do on the 30th she was relieved by HMAS *Condamine*. On 2nd November she supported UN troops from Sunwi-do who raided the mainland. Her time was drawing to a close with her last patrol being off Yongpyong-do until 5 November. In November she sailed for Sasebo then Hong Kong, then for home being relieved by HMCS *Haida*.

HMCS Crusader. Courtesy Public Archives Canada.

Canadian Crescent Class Destroyer
HMCS *Crusader*

HMCS	COMMENCED	COMPLETED	BUILDER
Crusader	1943	1945	John Brown

Displacement	1,710 tons Full load 2,525 tons
Dimensions	Length: 362¾ feet Beam: 35¾ feet Draught: 13¾ feet (mean)
Armament – gun	4 (single) 4.5" DP at A, B, X and Y positions
	4 × 2 pdr AA
	2 × 40 mm AA
	2 × 20 mm AA
Torpedo Tubes	4 (quad) 21"

Machinery	Geared turbines 40,000 shp to 2 shafts
Speed	33 knots
Fuel	580 tons oil fuel
Range	2800 nm at 20 knots
Complement	165 (peace)

HMCS	**IN THEATRE**	**TO**
Crusader	June 1952	June 1953

Korean Service

HMCS *Crusader* relieved *Athabaskan* on 21 June, 1952 and commenced inshore patrolling in the Cho-do area with gunfire support for the USN minesweepers *Redhead* and *Swallow* off Changsan-got Pt with intermittent bombardments in between. On 22 July she was relieved and sailed for Kure. For periods in September, *Crusader* with *Nootka* patrolled the inshore channels off Cho-do where the incident of the men in the inflated tubes occurred (see *Nootka* above).

Crusader relieved *Iroquois* on 14 October and patrolled the line from Songjin to Chaho for the rest of the month,with many bombardments and after dark escorting the minesweepers known as the Yang-do group, also anti-infiltration patrol through the islands by Songjin. In December *Crusader* was again on the inshore patrols during a period of bad weather and on 5/6 December was approached by four aircraft which she had detected on radar and opened fire. They bombed Cho-do and Sok-do but to little effect. On 10 December she was screening the USS *Baedong Strait* for over a week and on the 18th she sailed for Kure, to share Christmas with *Haida* and *Athabaskan.*

Crusader was at sea from 1 January, 1953 on the routine patrols and from 28 January to 9 February with *Athabaskan* was targeting the coastal railway which had a shortage of trains. On her last day she attacked motor transport on the coast road at Yang-do with enemy casualties and wrecked vehicles. She was then relieved by HMS *Cockade* and sailed to Sasebo.

During April *Crusader* was on the east coast. Her patrol commenced on the 9th and en route she found and sank a mine. By 11 April she was off Yang-do for a few days patrolling to Chongjin searching for would-be prisoners for intelligence purposes. On the 14th she was south of Tanchon eyeing the coastal railway and the following day destroyed a freight train less the locomotive which was uncoupled and escaped into a tunnel. She destroyed over 15 boxcars and in the morning handed over to a CAG to complete the job whilst she headed south to RAS. She was back on the 16th and caught two trains, one after the other, the second on a more inland line near Tanchon. She continued her task by bombardment until dark leaving little which would run again, and found and sank a mine with one of her 40 mm. She had to

115

screen the USN carrier for a short time but by the 20th was back at Yang-do, then moving to support I ROK Corps with the USS *St Paul*. Back again on the 24th she missed one train because the line curved inland below Songjin but later she severely damaged a locomotive and two cars by bombardment which resulted in a very large explosion leaving nothing at all for her to see. She had two more days offshore and on the 27th was relieved by HMS *Cockade* and made her course to Japan.

From 4th to 12th June, 1953 HMCS *Crusader* was screening the two carriers HMS *Glory* and the USS *Bairoko* off the west coast, with two detached periods off Cho-do giving gunfire support to the minesweepers off Sok-do and bombarding batteries at the Walsa-ri peninsula with HMNS *Johan Maurits van Nassau*. On the 12th she was relieved by *Athabaskan* and sailed for home via Sasebo.

HMCS Sioux. Courtesy Public Archives Canada.

Canadian 'V' Class Destroyer HMCS *Sioux*

HMCS	COMMENCED	COMPLETED	BUILDER
Sioux (ex *Vixen*)	1942	1944	White

Displacement	1,730 tons Full load 2,530 tons
Dimensions	Length: 362¾ feet Beam: 35¾ feet Draught: 13 feet (mean)
Armament – gun	2 (single) LA 4.7" in A and B positions
	4 × 40 mm AA
	2 × 20 mm AA
Torpedo Tubes	8 (2 quad) 21"
Anti-submarine	1 Squid
Machinery	Geared turbines 40,000 shp to 2 shafts
Speed	34 knots

Fuel	580 tons oil fuel
Range	2,800 nm at 20 knots
Complement	230

HMCS	**IN THEATRE**	**TO**
Sioux	July 1950	January 1951
	April 1951	February 1952

Korean Service

HMCS *Sioux* arrived at Sasebo on 30 July 1950 and was assigned to escort duties between Japan and Pusan. For a short period she was deployed for rescue duties but on 12th August she sailed with *Athabaskan* to the West Coast Support Group

She was employed in the west coast islands bombarding batteries, OPs and other targets and supporting landings of ROK troops on NK-controlled islands. On the 20th *Sioux* bombarded an island in the Popsong-po area and, with *Cayuga* bombarded the enemy at Taebu-do on 24 August, both returning to screen HMS *Triumph* and patrol in the Inchon and Kusan areas.

Sioux with *Ceylon* intercepted junks and sampans and destroyed four mines and bombarded Ongjin Pando peninsula. On 14 September *Sioux* was off Kunsan blockading but was relieved by *Cayuga* on the 17th to take up escort duties. She was still on the west coast in October escorting supply ships and screening HMS *Theseus*. From mid-December to early January, 1951 she was almost continuously off the west coast with periods on the carrier screen. On the 2nd January HMCS *Sioux* returned to Sasebo and returned to Canada two weeks later. She was back in theatre for April and relieved HMCS *Athabaskan* who sailed home on 3 May.

On 20 May *Sioux* was part of the force which supported Royal Marines landing on the mainland opposite Chodo, SIC were *Ceylon* and *Kenya*, *Sioux* bombarded the beaches detonating mines which might have hindered the Marines, then lifted her sights inland as the force advanced. *Sioux* relieved *Nootka* on 4 June and commenced operating in the swept channels with constant fire on such targets as appeared. She proceeded north to join in the siege of Wonsan bombarding several targets on the harbour and the Hodo peninsula, this being 14 June. The USS *Frank E. Evans* was in company and received enemy fire. *Sioux* returned to Wonsan on 17 June and was soon bombarding batteries at Kalma Pando and Umido. She had some effect as her gunnery set off a tremendous explosion on Umido. The Wonsan batteries were difficult to engage as most of the guns were positioned in caves. *Sioux* and ships in company bombarded through the night leaving her low on main ammunition.

On 18 June she had four near-misses with shell fragments hitting the ship but no casualties or damage. She again used up all her main ammunition except proximity-fused rounds. She was relieved the following day by *Whitesand Bay* and sailed for

Sasebo, then proceeded to HM Dockyard Hong Kong where her boilers were inspected and found to be in poor condition, so she remained in the dockyard until 24 August. On 25 August *Sioux* sailed for theatre off the west coast but had a quiet time until the 31st. In early September *Athabaskan*, *Cayuga* and *Sioux* spent some time on the carrier screen, then she had a further period in Sasebo. During November she was again screening but had three days patrolling, and for the last two weeks of the month, took part in bombarding Hungnam, Wonsan and Chongjin, expending 400 rounds of 4.7" ammunition at road targets and the coastal railway. On the 28th she was relieved and arrived at Kure on 30 November. In December *Sioux* operated off Cho-do which she reached on the 11th, she had a few uneventful days but on the 15/16th while guarding Sok-do, NK troops were firing on Chongyang-do and Ung-do. She provided counter battery fire with starshell but she was really firing blind so after anchoring a party of five boarded ROKN vessel 301 to reconnoitre, finding Ung-do was safe but Chanyang-do had fallen.

The following day she evacuated refugees and the wounded from Ung-do, *Sioux* engaged the mortars at Wolsa-ri and was assisted by HMS *Constance*. *Sioux*'s party returned safe and she left the area in the morning. For the remainder of the month she continued on the carrier screen. In January, 1952 she was on the west coast inshore patrol. From 29 January she was day after day bombarding gun and mortar positions with the USS *Porterfield* in company. During this patrol on 8 February *Sioux* was requested to send her medical officer to Cho-do where a US serviceman required urgent medical care. Due to ice along the shore, she could not use her boat, so an improvised flight deck was constructed of timber and other materials on board *Sioux* and a helicopter with the patient landed safely, the case was appendicitis. *Sioux* retired to the south and transferred the patient to HMS *Ceylon*. On 11 February she bombarded bunkers on the mainland opposite Cho-do and expended her 3,570th shell. With this bombardment she proceeded southward and arrived at Sasebo the following day, shortly leaving for home.

HMNZS Hawea. Courtesy Royal New Zealand Navy.

HMNZS Kaniere. Courtesy Royal New Zealand Navy.

HMNZS Pukaki. Courtesy Royal New Zealand Navy.

HMNZS Rotoiti. Courtesy Royal New Zealand Navy.

HMNZS Taupo. Courtesy Royal New Zealand Navy.

HMNZS Tutira. Courtesy Royal New Zealand Navy.

New Zealand Loch Class Frigates

———

HMNZS	COMMENCED	COMPLETED	BUILDER
Hawea (ex *Loch Eck*)	1943	1944	Smiths Dock
Kaniere (ex *Loch Achray*)	1943	1945	Smiths Dock
Pukaki (ex *Loch Achanalt*, ex *Naver*)	1943	1944	Henry Robb
Rotoiti (ex *Loch Katrine*)	1943	1944	Henry Robb
Taupo (ex *Loch Shin*)	1943	1944	Swan Hunter
Tutira (ex *Loch Morlich*)	1943	1944	Swan Hunter

Displacement	1,435 tons Full load 2,260 tons
Dimensions	Length: 307½ feet Beam: 38¾ feet Draught: 12 feet (mean)
Armament – gun	1 (single) DP 4" in A position
	4 × 2 pdr AA
	6 × 20 mm AA
Anti submarine	2 Squids
Machinery	Triple expansion 5,500 ihp to 2 shafts
Speed	18 knots
Fuel	724 tons oil fuel
Complement	114

HMNZS	IN THEATRE	TO	MILES STEAMED	AMMUNITION EXPENDITURE
Hawea	March 1951	January 1952	55,000	21,000
	August 1952	Armistice	38,000	3,981
Kaniere	March 1953	Armistice	13,984	4,400
Pukaki	July 1950	December 1950	30,000	?
Rotoiti	October 1950	November 1951	51,000	12,700
	January 1952	March 1953	58,000	13,400
Taupo	August 1951	October 1952	58,200	16,044
Tutira	July 1950	May 1951	35,400	?

Korean Service

There were always two RNZN frigates on station from the commencement to completion of the war.

HMNZS *Hawea* entered theatre on 26 April, 1951 at a period when the land fighting had stabilised. On 18 May she patrolled the area off Cho-do and found a target, fired 29 rounds and secured three hits. Two days later she supported Royal Marine Commandos, who were to raid in three LCVPs from HMS *Ceylon*. She bombarded the beaches to destroy land mines, later shifting fire as the raid progressed. On 26 July she joined the operation within the Han estuary and used her communication suite for the benefit of the accompanying frigates. She also bombarded the west bank of the Haeju-man and continued with the communications task but in 18/24 August was interrupted by typhoon Marge, and anchored for almost four days. On 23 November she proceeded to Cho-do to relieve HMNZS *Taupo*, and assisted a guerilla landing on the mainland, then sailed to Sok-do with *Cayuga* in company. On 25 August *Hawea* returned to the Han, proceeding through the narrow channels and eventually spending 23 days there and steaming 350 miles in those restricted waters. On 21 September being 16 miles inside she engaged troop concentrations and landed a party of 13 men to set up an OP on an island three miles distant, but only one mile from the target. She fired 50 rounds before the OP was noticed by the enemy, who commenced mortar fire and the party returned on board. She continued with the usual patrols and on 3 February 1952 left Kure for home, she had been away 371 days with 272 days at sea, steamed 55,000 miles and fired 21,000 rounds of ammunition.

When she returned from New Zealand she spent 24 hours in harbour, then rejoined the west coast ships. On 26 November, she was visited by the Minister of Defence, T.L. MacDonald. Her routine brought her into port for Christmas Day, which she spent in Sasebo. On 7 January 1953, she was off Taedong-man, that night being off Wollae-do, a 76 mm battery opened fire and *Hawea* straight away replied.

Her next patrol when off Taedong-man had a surprising incident, her asdic operator reported a possible submarine, the frigate went to depth charge (squid) attack with oil coming to the surface, but on investigation it proved to be the wreck of a 1,300-ton Japanese ship sunk in 1944. On 4 March 1953 a concentration of NK troops was observed on Yang-do. The target being out of range, she called up a CAS and controlled the action, stating in her log 'that by 1400, the enemy were dealt with'. On her next patrol, she supported a further landing but was troubled by a battery of 76 mm guns, positioned in caves, the closest shell landed 15 yards away. She was relieved by HMNZS *Kaniere* and proceeded to Kure, taking part in the Coronation Day parade on 2 June 1953. She was back on patrol in early June, and on the 11 June and for days later, bombarding shore positions and mortar sites but also supervising the stream of junks, bringing civilians from the disputed islands. On 28 July came the cease fire.

HMNZS *Kaniere* arrived at Sasebo on 23 April, 1953 and the following day left for the west coast of Korea, appropriately enough she entered theatre on 25 April, which is ANZAC Day. She commenced supporting minesweeping operations and evacuation of wounded from various points. She proceeded to the Han and took over from *Hawea* attacking mortar positions, troop concentrations, bunkers and an ammunition dump, demolishing an NK mess hall which was occupied at the time. She was in Kure on 2 June 1953 and took part in the Coronation Day parade. By 10 June she was back in the operational area and shortly after supervised an evacuation of partisans from Cho-do. She was engaged by two batteries but moved out of range, but not before firing 20 rounds in return. On 28 July, 1953 the cease fire came into force.

HMNZS *Pukaki* sailed from Auckland on 3 July arriving on the 19th in theatre and took on war stores, etc. On arrival in Sasebo she was escorting convoys to Pusan with *Black Swan*. They sailed from Sasebo in the afternoon, arrived at Pusan in the early hours of the following morning, patrolled off the harbour, then returned to Japan at full speed. On 12 September she left Pusan with a convoy for Inchon, escorting the allied ships to the beaches, and on 10 October left for Wonsan, in company were *Mounts Bay* and the French ship *La Grandiere*. They arrived off Wonsan on 20 October but there was no swept channel to the beaches. In consequence the US Marines sarcastically dubbed this as operation Yo-Yo as they steamed south for 12 hours and then northward for 12 hours. On 26 October, the troops could finally land. *Pukaki* was on a patrol line 100 miles long and sighted and sank a floating mine. She proceeded to Kure, arriving there on 4 November, 1950, being relieved by HMNZS *Tutira*.

HMNZS *Rotoiti* arrived on the same day as *Tutira* at Sasebo. *Rotoiti* proceeded to the west coast of Korea and was deployed to control traffic at Chinnampo and Inchon, and escort ships between those ports. At this period floating mines were a constant problem and a sharp lookout had to be maintained. The route inshore between Changsangot and Cho-do was unsafe for the larger ships, excepting when operationally necessary, until further sweeping had been carried out. At the end of 1950 *Rotoiti* remained off the west coast, alternating with periods at Kure, Tokyo or Sasebo. Frozen seas appeared with falling snow and bad visibility. In February and until April, *Rotoiti* was engaged on escort and patrols. One incident occurred after she had relieved *Hawea* on 17 July, 1951 and to quote from the official history of the Korean War, by the Government of Korea, 'HMNZS *Rotoiti* became engaged with one of the most brilliant raids during the war. She was steaming past Sogon-ni Pt, 15 miles south of Cho-do in the outer approaches to Chinnampo harbour when her signalman noticed a tree which seemed to have grown since the frigate's last visit there. Further examination disclosed figures in uniform moving around its base. The CO decided to raid the position. The conditions seemed favourable since ships had frequently come under machine gun fire from the point and just as frequently had bombarded in return. It seemed probable therefore that the enemy had developed the habit of moving undercover during a bombardment and could safely be sent there while an assault group landed. The position was located on a cliff which jutted out into deep water and the face of the cliff fell away in a landslide to a beach and it appeared from the ship that this could be scaled. Some of *Rotoiti's* ship's company had been trained in beach landing tactics and a platoon was formed consisting of 14 men under the command of an officer. Within minutes, the raid was underway and under cover of a bombardment, the assault platoon left the ship. As the boat reached the beach, the raiders surrounded the position and the assault team of two able seamen climbed the landslide at the double with covering fire from the ship. They swept over the cliff, reached the position, shot an NK soldier who had a grenade ready and took prisoner two more who were hiding in a foxhole. They shepherded the prisoners down the cliff under rifle fire, covering fire from the ship protected the party during its embarkation and returned to the frigate. The boat was hoisted on board and the prisoners examined one hour after the operation began'.

In August she relieved *Morecambe Bay* in the Han and steamed upstream to bombard Yonan from the south-east and northward up the Yesong river. On the 17th 400 NK troops appeared on the riverbank and were quickly engaged leaving many casualties. Typhoon Marge came and went with *Rotoiti* anchored four days off Inchon. Later *Rotoiti* proceeded to Cho-do Sok-do patrol and raid mission with the Royal Marines. This took place in darkness and two boats were launched for the assault party to the beaches, but enemy troops were waiting and a firefight ensued, with one able seaman being killed. Until early September *Rotoiti* remained in this area which was rather uneventful. On 2 September she was relieved by HMCS *Cayuga* to return to New Zealand.

During her passage home, she received a distress signal from the British ship SS *Hupeh* which had been attacked and seized by pirates off the mouth of the Yangtse. She altered course and soon detected the ship which was identified as the *Hupeh*. There were 49 armed pirates who threatened to shoot the officers, women and children if *Rotoiti* attempted to board. *Rotoiti*'s CO appreciated the dire situation and soon the pirates made an offer, if they were promised safe custody to a nearby island, they would respect the safety of the officers, passengers and cargo. It was a difficult decision for the CO to make, but after taking all into consideration, safe custody was agreed, the pirates were put ashore and the *Hupeh* continued to Hong Kong.

On 3 February, 1952 *Hawea* was relieved by *Rotoiti* commencing her second tour, having left New Zealand on 7 January. Back to the old routine, to the Han river, bombardments and supporting another raid. It was found the batteries ashore were now heavier than previously and access to the upper reaches could not be continued. *Rotoiti* continued escort and blockade on the west coast. She bombarded as required and during this action one of her cooks became ill with appendicitis, but was operated on satisfactorily. She was relieved by *Taupo* near Paengnyong-do and returned to Sasebo then to Hong Kong for maintenance. Back off the coastline the usual patrols continued with bombardments, screening and evacuation of casualties. She returned to Kure in October and was inspected by the First Sea Lord, Admiral Sir Rhoderick McGrigor. *Rotoiti* was in port for Christmas at Kure, but sailed on Boxing Day to the Cho-do area. Again routine patrols and on 28 February she left Sasebo homeward bound for New Zealand.

HMNZS *Taupo* relieved *Rotoiti* having arrived at Sasebo on 29 August, 1951. She was soon involved in the routine and sailed for the Han river where she was involved in spotting targets for shore bombardment and surveyed the bombardment anchorage. That month she was on convoy escort duty on the Cho-do Sok-do route also patrolling the Haeju area. On 23 November she was relieved by *Hawea* off Cho-do. She had patrolled as far north as Taehwa-do but with little enemy response.

On 1st December she was engaging the coastal railway and attempted blocking railway tunnels, *Hawea* was in company on this occasion. In February, 1952 *Taupo* was off the east coast patrolling the Songjin area with the Yang-do group of islands to the north-east. She was looking for trains but learnt Yang-do was under fire with an enemy raid imminent. Proceeding at best possible speed she saw 15 troop-carrying sampans, engaged and sank 10. The USS *Endicott* and *Shelton* were in support but the batteries were giving heavy fire while those that were left of the invaders were returning to the mainland. She was in a two-mile-wide strait and a near miss penetrated *Taupo*'s engine-room with other fire close to port and under her bows. The light increased and the batteries threatened and in consequence she withdrew from that location. The same day she gave medical aid to treat casualties on Yang-do embarking some wounded for transfer to the USS *St Paul* and continued her patrol until 27 February. Some days later she demolished by gunfire two rebuilt enemy bridges, stood by Yang-do Island, continued to patrol and returned to Sasebo on 27 February, 1952. *Taupo* also visited Hong Kong for R&R on 14 April.

On 1 May she sailed again to enter theatre monitoring the change of garrison between friendly islands in the Cho-do and Sok-do area. Some enemy activity was expected and contact was maintained with the USS *Craig* regarding NK troop-carrying junks and sampans near the Ongjin peninsula which had been invaded. Cho-do was alerted and one enemy was taken prisoner. Later *Taupo* steamed to meet *Belfast* on similar duties and delivered mail. An unexpected duty was dealing with outbreaks of typhus on Cho-do and Paengnyong-do by the medical team from *Taupo*.

On 9 September 1952 HMNZS *Taupo* relieved *Rotoiti* near Paengnyong-do, patrolled and bombarded and on 17 September returned to Sasebo on her homeward way to New Zealand.

HMNZS *Tutira* sailed with *Pukaki* on 3 July 1950 and arrived in theatre via Hong Kong then continued their journey to Sasebo. They were deployed to escort duties of convoys from Japan to Pusan for some weeks but on 12 September 1950 they left for the Inchon landings, still as convoy escorts. The two frigates then sailed for Wonsan arriving on 20 October 1950 and encountered Operation Yo-Yo mentioned previously. *Tutira* was then ordered to Kure where *Rotoiti* arrived on 4 November. She went with *Rotoiti* back to the west coast and was responsible for controlling traffic entering Chinnampo and Inchon with escort duties also. In March, 1951 *Tutira* was senior ship off Paengnyong-do working with ROKN minesweepers. *Tutira* became well-known to the smaller ships of the Republic of Korea Navy and the three weeks involved were stated to be 'most interesting'. At the conclusion *Tutira* refitted at Kure and returned home to New Zealand being relieved by HMNZS *Hawea*.

RASCV Reginald Kerr under Army command from the Royal Navy. Her bow door and a 'bone in her teeth' are well shown. Photograph courtesy of the Imperial War Museum, London. (Neg. no. FL18185)

Royal Army Service Corps
Landing Ships (Tank)

RASCV	LAUNCHED	COMPLETED	BUILDER
Maxwell Brander (ex L 3024)	1944	1945	Smith's Dock
Frederick Clover (ex L 3001)	1945	1945	Vickers Armstrong (Tyne)
Reginald Kerr (ex L 3009)	1944	1945	Harland & Wolff
Charles Macleod (ex L 3021)	1944	1945	Lithgows (Port Glasgow)

Displacement   4,820 tons loaded   3,065 tons beaching

Armament – guns   4 (twin) 20 mm DP AA
       (as built)   2 (single) 20 mm DP AA

Dimensions	Length: 346 feet Beam: 54 feet
	Draught: 4⅞ feet forward 11½ feet aft
Machinery	Triple expansion of 2,750 ihp to each of two shafts
Speed	13½ knots
Range	8,000 nm at 11knots
Complement	104

Notes: These were four Landing Ships (Tank) Mark 3 transferred to the Royal Army Service Corps among many others from the Royal Navy, virtually as new buildings.

Korean Service

All arrived in theatre after December 1950 and despite being sold to the North Atlantic Shipping Co., later British India Steam Navigation Co., all remained tasked to the Army's needs in and out of theatre. They were based at Kure, but made many voyages to various Korean ports.

Republic of Colombia
Almirante Padilla Class Frigates

———

ARC	COMMENCED	COMPLETED	BUILDER
Almirante Brion (ex USS *Burlington*)	1943	1944	Consolidated Steel, Los Angeles
Almirante Padilla (ex USS *Groton*)	1943	1944	Walter Butler, Wisconsin
Capitan Tono (ex USS *Bisbee*)	1943	1944	Consolidated Steel, Los Angeles

Displacement	1,430 tons Full load 2,100 tons but *Capitan Tono* 2,200 tons
Dimensions	Length: 303½ feet Beam: 37½ feet Draught: 13¾ feet
Armament – gun	3 (single) 3" DP/AA 50 cal at A, B and X posns
Anti submarine	1 Hedgehog
	6 depth charge throwers
	2 depth charge racks
Machinery	Triple expansion giving 5,500 ihp to two shafts
Speed	20 knots
Complement	*Almirante Brion* 120
	Almirante Padilla 147
	Capitan Tono 103

Design note: All ex US Navy built and designed patrol frigates derived from the RN River Class

ARC	IN THEATRE	TO
Almirante Brion	June 1953	April 1954
Almirante Padilla	May 1951	February 1952
	March 1955	October 1955
Capitan Tono	April 1952	January 1953
	April 1954	March 1955

Korean Service

ARC *Almirante Brion* arrived in theatre in June, 1953 and was hardly inducted into the ways of the WCSG before the Armistice was signed, however she remained in theatre carrying out missions as allocated.

ARC *Almirante Padilla* was in theatre by May 1951 and commenced inshore patrols off the west coast. On 14 June she moved to the east coast and bombarded Wonsan and Songjin also on special missions, conveying ROK agents from Yodo Island to Songjin. This was a busier task than may have been expected and it was not until January 1952 that she was bombarding the coastal railway between Songjin and Hungnam. Also the railway between Chongjin to Hungnam was bombarded with damaging effects on the NK rail system. On 19 January ARC *Almirante Padilla* returned to Colombia.

ARC *Capitan Tono* entered theatre in April 1952 having been relieved by ARC *Almirante Padilla* at Yokosuka on her homeward way. By May 1952 *Capitan Tono* was off the east coast escorting convoys for the UN forces, also bombardment and patrols were carried out. On 19 May she proceeded north to Wonsan, bombarding there and off Songjin until the end of August then after R&R for two weeks at Sasebo, back to escorting UN convoys and the heavier ships of the USN. On 12 November she steamed to Yokosuka and from there on 27 January 1953 sailed back to Colombia.

HDMS Jutlandia. Courtesy East Asiatic Company.

Kingdom of Denmark Hospital Ship *Jutlandia*

In August 1950 the Danish Government decided that one of the most practical ways to assist the Republic of Korea was to offer the use of a hospital ship, which was gratefully accepted. The ship chosen was the *Jutlandia* of the Danish East Asiatic Company which had been in the passenger trade but was converted into a hospital ship on behalf of the Danish Government and operated by the Danish Red Cross organisation.

On 23 January 1951 HDMS *Jutlandia* sailed from Denmark and arrived in theatre on 7 March, 1951. She served as a sanctuary for the wounded and dying of both sides that were transferred to her. She returned home on 24 July 1951 for rotation of crew and replenishment of supplies.

The second tour was from 29 September 1951 to 29 March 1952, with a third tour from 20 September 1952 to 16 October 1953. During her service over 15,000 patients received treatment on board with only 25 deaths. Throughout the periods mentioned, the significance of the Red Cross organisation came to mean quite a lot to those who were involved in the war and the people of Korea.

RFS Dixmude, ex-HMS Biter, escort aircraft carrier. Courtesy J. W. Goss.

Republic of France Escort Carrier *Dixmude*

———

RFS	COMPLETED	BUILDER
Dixmude (ex HMS *Biter*, ex *Rio Parana*)	1940	Sun SB & DD Co., Chester, Pa.

Displacement	8,200 tons Full load 15,500 tons
Dimensions	Length: 496 feet Beam: 69½ feet Draught: 25½ feet
Armament – gun	3 (single) 4" AA
	19 × 20 mm AA on single and twin mountings
Aircraft	Fixed and folding wing up to 30
Machinery	Diesel electric of 8,500 bhp to 1 shaft
Speed	16½ knots
Range	20,000 nm at 15 knots
Lifts	2 no
Complement	403

Originally the mercantile MV *Rio Parana* but converted in WW II.

Korean Service

Volume 6 of *History of UN Forces In Korean War* does not mention the above escort carrier but it is understood that she sailed from France with urgently needed aircraft and spares to the Korean War zone, discharged and then left for French Indo-China, which was itself at this period in turmoil.

RFS La Grandiere. Courtesy Musee de la Marine.

Republic of France
First Class Sloop – Minelaying Type

―――

RFS	COMPLETED	BUILDER
La Grandière (ex Ville D'Ys)	1939	Ch., Provence

Displacement	1,969 tons Full load 2,600 tons
Dimensions	Length: 340 feet Beam: 41¾ feet Draught: 14¼ feet
Armament – gun	3 (single) 5.5"
	4 × 40 mm AA
	11 × 20 mm AA on single and twin mountings
Mines	Up to 40 according to type
Machinery	Sulzer diesels to two shafts giving 3,200 bhp
Speed	15½ knots
Range	13,000 nm at 8½ knots and 7,600 nm at 15 knots
Fuel	325 tons oil fuel and 60 tons of boiler fuel
Complement	135 to 194 according to task

Class note: one of a class of four (*Charner* class) all completed prior to WWII and built for tropical service and fitted for flag use.

Korean Service
La Grandière sailed from France and arrived in Sasebo on 29 July 1950 and became an operational unit with the Task Force. She served on the outer screen during the Inchon landings, and later escorted the Minesweeping Element on the East coast before being withdrawn.

HMNS Evertsen. Courtesy Afdeling Maritieme.

HMNS Piet Hein. Courtesy Afdeling Maritieme.

Royal Netherlands
Navy Evertsen Class Destroyers

HMNS	**COMPLETED**	**BUILDER**
Evertsen (ex *Scourge*)	1942	Cammell Laird
Piet Hein (ex *Serapis*)	1943	Scotts

Displacement	1,796 tons Full load 2,528 tons
Dimensions	Length: 362¾ feet Beam: 35¾ feet Draught: 10 feet
Armament – gun	4 (single) 4.7" DP
	8 × 20 mm AA on single or twin mountings
Torpedo Tubes	8 (quad) 21"
Machinery	Geared turbines to 2 shafts giving 40,000 shp
Speed	31 knots
Complement	232

HMNS	**IN THEATRE**	**TO**
Evertsen	July 1950	April 1951
Piet Hein	March 1952	January 1953

Korean Service

HMNS *Evertsen* entered the operational theatre on 16 July 1950 and was initially incorporated in TU 96.8.2, but later in July the east and west coast groups were consolidated into TG 96.5.

By August 1950 *Evertsen* was bombarding off Inchon with the USS *Sicily* and other allied vessels in preparation for the Inchon landing on 15 September. *Evertsen* was with other destroyers in the task of close and outer screen duties, operating off Inchon. By February 1951 she was again off Wonsan and in March assisting the siege off Hungnam.

HMNS *Piet Hein* entered theatre on 26 August 1952 supporting a guerilla raid on Sunmi-do. In the period to 28 September 1952 she was screening *Ocean* and on 15 October she bombarded in the Chodo area. Until 18 January 1953 she was deployed on the east coast with other allied ships and participated in bombarding trains as they emerged from tunnels and so damaging the NK war effort. She was relieved by HMNS *Johan Maurits van Nassau*.

HMNS Van Galen. Courtesy Afdeling Maritieme.

Royal Netherlands Navy Destroyer *Van Galen*

HMNS	COMPLETED	BUILDER
Van Galen (ex HMS *Noble*)	1940	Denny

Displacement	1,760 tons Full load 2,523 tons
Dimensions	Length: 348 feet Beam: 35 feet Draught: 9 feet (mean)
Armament – gun	6 (twin) 4.7" LA in shields
	4 × 40 mm AA in single or twin mtgs
	6 × 20 mm AA in single or twin mtgs
Torpedo Tubes	10 (2 quin) 21"
Machinery	Geared turbines to 2 shafts giving 40,000 shp
Speed	31 knots
Fuel	500 tons of fuel oil
Complement	246

HMNS	**IN THEATRE**	**TO**
Van Galen	April 1951	March 1952

Korean Service

HMNS *Van Galen* entered theatre in April 1951 relieving *Evertsen*, and commenced operations with the WCSG and in April 1951 was present at the siege of Hungnam with much bombarding. In July she was screening the USS carriers *Bataan* and later *Sicily* off the west coast but concentrating on the coastline to the north.

Later in October *Van Galen* relieved *Concord* off the east coast where she bombarded between Wonsan, Songjin and Hamhung. The next month she was present at an air and sea strike against Hungnam with *Belfast* and *Tobruk* also bombarding with airstrikes by aircraft from *Sydney*. In December she had returned to the west coast and relieved *Athabaskan* then taking part in the operations off the islands. She was relieved by *Piet Hein* in March 1952 and sailed home to the Netherlands.

HMNS Johan Maurits Van Nassau. Courtesy Afdeling Maritieme.

Royal Netherlands Navy
Frigate *Johan Maurits van Nassau*

HMNS	COMPLETED	BUILDER
Johan Maurits van Nassau	1943	Simons
(ex HMS *Ribble*)		

Displacement	1,463 tons Full load 1,994 tons
Dimensions	Length: 301½ feet Beam: 36½ feet Draught: 14¼ feet
Armament – gun	2 (single) 4.1" DP/AA
	7 × 20 mm on single or twin mountings
Machinery	Triple expansion of 5,500 ihp to two shafts
Speed	20 knots
Fuel	440 tons of oil fuel
Complement	120

HMNS	**IN THEATRE**	**To**
Johan Maurits van Nassau	January 1953	November 1953

Korean Service

HMNS *Johan Maurits van Nassau* entered theatre in January, 1953 and was deployed to the routines and tasks of the WCSG. The early months of 1953 were stormy and like the Arctic, perhaps reducing the naval activity, but in May with other UN ships she was bombarding the newly-established batteries on the Amgak peninsula and other targets as required, with many batteries being hit also trains on the coastal railway. She guarded the many islands in company of *Crusader* and supported the ROKN minesweepers off Sok-to, then came the cease-fire but she remained in Korean waters in case of any eventuality until relieved on 5 December 1953 when she sailed for home.

HMTS Bangpakong, sister ship to the earlier Prasae. Courtesy Royal Thai Navy.

Royal Thai Navy Prasae Class
Anti-Submarine Frigates

HMTS	COMPLETED	BUILDER
Prasae (ex *Sind*, ex *Betony*)	1943	A. Hall
Bangpakong (ex *Gondwana*, ex *Burnet*)	1943	Ferguson

Displacement	1,060 tons Full load 1,350 tons
Dimensions	Length: 203¼ feet Beam: 33 feet Draught: 13¾ feet
Armament – gun	1(single) 4" DP AA
	7 × 20 mm DP AA on single or twin mtgs
Anti submarine	6 depth charge throwers
Machinery	Triple expansion of 2880 ihp to one shaft
Speed	16 knots
Fuel	282 tons of oil fuel
Complement	101

Gunnery note: these vessels were ex RN corvettes of the Flower Class and had seen at least two years of hard service in WWII. It is said their 4" gun barrels may have been a little worn.

HMTS	IN THEATRE	TO
Prasae	November 1950	January 1951
Bangpakong	November 1950	February 1952

Korean Service

These ships of the Royal Thai Navy were from quite early on in the war engaged in bombardments of the NK forces batteries, logistics areas, the coastal railway and other targets as designated. In January 1951 HMTS *Prasae*, *Bangpakong* and the USS *English* were in very bad weather with heavy snow and gales. On the 7th off Yangyang with a lee shore *Prasae* went aground being abandoned about a week later, and despite efforts at salvage by ships of the UN Force nothing could move her. Therefore in order to prevent sensitive equipment, etc. being taken by the North Koreans she was shelled and set on fire by the guns of the USS *English*.

HMTS *Bangpakong* continued with the blockade escort and mining group and operated off Wonsan harbour against enemy batteries. Later in May she continued to serve on similar tasks and in June 1951 was in company with the USS *Gloucester* bombarding gun positions and installations at Yongdong-ni and Kalma-kap.

Bangpakong was then deployed to escorting oilers of the USN. In September she was in action off Wonsan and Songjin on an almost continuous patrol. She left Wonsan on 21st October 1951 for a period of R&R, returning to the gunline in November finally being relieved by HMTS *Prasae II* and *Tachin* on 29 December 1951 returning to Thailand by 16 February 1952.

HMTS Prasae (II), operational off Korea. Courtesy Royal Thai Navy.

HMTS Tachin, sister ship to the Prasae (II). Clearly shown are the unshielded 3" guns at 'A' and 'B' positions with a single 20mm AA on the starboard lower bridge wing. Courtesy Royal Thai Navy.

Royal Thai Navy
Prasae Class Patrol Frigates

———

HMTS	COMMENCED	COMPLETED	BUILDER
Prasae (II) (ex *Gallup*)	1943	1944	Consolidated Steel, Los Angeles
Tachin (ex *Glendale*)	1943	1943	Consolidated Steel, Los Angeles

Displacement	1,430 tons Full load 2,100 tons
Dimensions	Length: 304 feet Beam: 37½ feet Draught: 13¾ feet
Armament – gun	3 (single) 3" DP 50 cal
	10 × 40 mm AA on single and twin mtgs
	6 × 20 mm AA on single and twin mtgs
Anti submarine	6 depth charge throwers
Machinery	Triple expansion to 2 shafts giving 5,500 ihp
Speed	20 knots
Fuel	685 tons oil fuel
Range	9,500 nm at 12 knots
Complement	180

Note: were designed on the lines of the WWII Royal Navy River class.

HMTS	IN THEATRE	TO
Prasae II	December 1951	January 1955
Tachin	December 1951	January 1955

Korean Service

HMTS *Prasae II* arrived at Sasebo on 26 December 1951 and on 11 January 1952 escorted an oiler, the USS *Taluga* with *Capitan Tono* off the east coast to RAS with other UN ships over a period of 12 days then returned to Sasebo. The following month she was again escorting an oiler off Wonsan returning to Sasebo on 16 February. On 5 April *Prasae II* relieved *Tachin* of escort duties in the Eastern Sea and directed the USS *Manatee* from Ullung-do to Songjin, then escorted the USS *Platte* to Sasebo.

In May the crew was rotated and on 5 June she sailed to relieve the USS *Burlington* off Ulling-do, returning to Sasebo on the 13th and continued escorting from the 21 to 30. In July 1953 steamed to Yokosuka for repair and maintenance. She continued escort duties for some months later.

HMTS *Tachin* arrived in theatre on the same date as *Prasae II* and sailed on their first patrol together. On 13 February 1952 *Tachin* again sailed on escort duties off Songjin and on the 17th was employed as picket vessel whilst the duty US destroyer sailed to RAS. She was off Songjin again on 2 March patrolling and bombarding off Songjin and picketing Mayang-do, on the 6th she was bombarding Wonsan then returned to Sasebo. By the 19th she was escorting transports being relieved by *Prasae II* on 5 April to escort the USS *Manatee*. By the 26th she was escorting the USS *Alatede* to Pusan and the following day back to Ullung-do. During May she was escorting including the USS *Mispillion* to Wonsan then returning with the USS *Cacapon* arriving in Sasebo on the 17th. She rotated her crew on the 30th and continued escorting for some months even after the Armistice in 1953 but she needed drydocking which commenced on 2 August at Sasebo.

HMTS Sichang, Naval Transport. Courtesy Royal Thai Navy.

Royal Thai Navy Naval Transport *Sichang*

HMTS	COMPLETED	BUILDER
Sichang	1938	Harima D Y

Displacement	815 tons
Dimensions	Length: 160 feet Beam: 28 feet Draught: 16 feet
Armament	2 × 20 mm DP AA on single mtgs
Machinery	Twin shaft diesel engines giving 550 bhp
Speed	16 knots
Complement	30

HMTS	IN THEATRE	TO
Sichang	November 1950	July 1951

Korean Service

HMTS *Sichang* entered theatre with *Prasae* and *Bangpakong* transporting a detachment of troops of the Royal Thai Army destined for the battlefields of Korea. The regiment was the 21st Royal Thai with other troops onboard the chartered ship *Hertamaersk* which was of Danish flag. En route to Korea the weather worsened and *Sichang* began to take on water having to put into Okinawa for repairs and re-victualling but finally arriving at Pusan on 7 November. At this period at Pusan she also was supplied with mixed fuel which was speedily found out and rectified. On 27 January she sailed with *Bangpakong* for Yokohama where the latter received replacement armament and modern radio equipment and *Sichang* had a general overhaul, returning to Sasebo on 19 April 1951 and sailing home to Thailand on 15 July 1951.

Appendix 1

The term task force regarding naval vessels may not be understood by some readers. Essentially the word 'fleet' could be used as in days long ago when the Royal Navy had an Atlantic Fleet, Home Fleet and a Mediterranean Fleet. Although such descriptions may still be used, since today more than one nation's vessels deploy and operate together, the words Task Force are the more appropriate term at sea. There is always more than one naval task force around the globe so each has a different number. On first arriving in Korea VA Joy, COMNAVFE allocated Admiral Andrewes with all Commonwealth and allied ships to be the West Korean Support Group TG 96.8, and RA Higgins with the USN ships to be the East Korean Support Group TG 96.5. For the special operation of the Inchon landings, the West Coast Support Group was augmented by vessels from other regions, and became Task Force 91. On 25th September, after the successful completion of the assault, TF 91 was dissolved and became Task Group 95.1, part of the UN Blockade and Escort Force, comprising about (for example) 60 ships with one Commander-in-Chief RA Smith USN who is CTF 95. Such a TF is large and unwieldy therefore for tactical purposes it was split in two creating two task groups which would be numbered Task Group 95.1 for the West Coast Support Group and Task Group 95.2 for the East Coast Support Group, which is again unwieldy. TG 95.1 was therefore split into five Task Elements according to the task of each:

> Task Element 95.11 Air patrol and blockade element: carrier and attached destroyers
>
> Task Element 95.12 Surface patrol and blockade element: cruisers and attached destroyers
>
> Task Element 95.13 Screen element: vessels detailed to protect landing craft or fleet replenishment vessels
>
> Task Element 95.14: Minesweeping Element: Minesweepers and escorting frigates
>
> Task Element 95.15: Inshore Element: ROK Naval vessels

Smaller units or individual vessels detached for a specific task are designated as Task Units, e.g. *Theseus* or whichever USN carrier rotated patrols with her would be TU 95. 11.1

To those not familiar with the above, the system may appear to be complex but it is flexible and has stood the test of time.

Appendix 2

_____

Korean Suffixes

bau (pau)	rock
bong (pong)	bong, pong or san denotes a mountain
chon	river, in general small river forming a tributary to Gang (e.g. Sami-chon joins the Imjin Gang)
dan (tan)	point
do (to)	island (e.g. Chejudo, Tokdo)
dong (tong)	village, settlement
gang (kang)	river (e.g. Han Gang, Naktong Gang)
gap (kap)	point
gol (kol)	village, ravine or valley
jae (chae)	mountain pass
li (ni, ri)	area name, smallest administrative unit consisting of several villages; township
lyong (nyong, ryong)	mountain or mountain pass
maul	village, settlement
nae	stream, creek or brook
namdo	south province
pukto (bugdo)	north province
sa	temple
san	mountain
yon	deep water or pool, abyss or swamp

Appendix 3

Casualties of the Naval Forces of the WCSG

	Royal Navy (officers)	Royal Navy (ratings)	Royal Marines (officers)	Royal Marines (other ranks)
Killed	25	15	1	17
Missing	1	–	1	1
Wounded	5	15	3	64
POW	2	2	–	20

	Royal Australian Navy	Royal Canadian Navy	Royal Thai Navy
Killed	1	3	2
Missing	2	–	–
Wounded	6	11	–
Disease	–	–	2

Extracted from *History of UN Forces in Korean War*, Vol VI, 1977.

Appendix 4

Locations mentioned in the text of West Coast Support Group

AMGAK	HANTAN	MIRYANG
AMNOK GANG	HO-DO	MU-DO
ANJU	HONGCHON	MUKHO
CHAHO	HUNGNAM	MUSUDAN Pt
CHAIL-LI	HYONPUNG	MYONGGI-SAN
CHANGDAN	HYON-NI	NAECHON
CHANGHOWAN	ICHON	NAKTONG
CHANGNIN-DO	IMJIN River	NAP-DO
CHANGSAN-GOT	INCHON	NOLBUNYO-RI
CHAGYAK-DO	KA-DO	OCHONG-DO
CHARIDAE	KAESON	OHWA-DO
CHASON	KALMA-BANDO	ONGJIN
CHASAN	KAMA-GOL	OSAN
CHINNAMPO	KAMAK-SAN	PAENGNYONG-DO
CHIPYONG-NI	KANGHWA-DO	PAKCHON
CHO-DO	KANGNUNG	PANMUMJON
CHOKSONG	KAPYONG	POCHON
CHOMI-DO	KASAN	POHANG
CHONGCHON River	KIMPO	PUKCHANG
CHONGJIN	KOBUK-SOM	PUKHAN
CHONGJU	KOJE-DO	PUKPYONG
CHONGPYONG	KOSONG	PUSAN
CHONGYANG-DO	KOTO-RI	PYONGGANG
CHORWON	KOWANG-SAN	PYONGTAEK
CHUAM-NI	KOYANG	PYONGYANG
CHUMUNJIN	KUMGONG-NI	SAMCHOK
CHUNGCHON-NI	KUMHWA	SAMI-CHON
HAEJU	KUMYANGJANG-NI	SARDIN
HAEJU-MAN	KUNSAN	SARIWON
HAGAL	KUNI-RI	SEOUL
HAGARU-RI	KYONGSONG-MAN	SIBYON-NI
HAMHUNG	MANPOJIN	SINANJU
HAMHURHAM	MARYANG-SAN	SIN-DO
HAN	MASOGU-RI	SINGYE

SINMI-DO
SINUIJU
SOCHONG-DO
SOK-TO
SOLMA-RI
SONGHWAN
SONGJIN
SONJU
SOSUAP-DO
SUKCHON
SUNCHON
SUNWI-DO
SUWON
TAECHON
TAECHANG
TAECHONG-DO
TAEDONG
TAEGU
TAEJON
TAERYONG

TAESUP-DO
TAEWHA-DO
TANCHON
TAN-DO
TOKCHOK-DO
TOKCHON
TOKCHONG
TONGDUCHON
U-DO
UIJONGBU
UNCHON
UNGDO
UNSAN
URI-DO
WAEGWAN
WOLLAE-DO
WOLMI-DO
WOLMUN-NI
WOLSA-RI
WONJU

WONSAN
YALU River
YANG-DO
YANGPYONG
YANGSU-RI
YO-DO
YOJU
YONCHON
YONGDONG
YONGDUNGPO
YONGMAE-DO
YONPYONG-DO
YONGYU
YONPO
YONSO-DONG
YOPA-RI
YOSU
YUK-TO

Appendix 5

Further details of dates in theatre for HM ships

HMS	IN THEATRE FROM	TO
Charity	July 1950	January 1951
	July 1951	September 1951
	December 1951	March 1952
	August 1952	November 1952
	February 1953	April 1953
	June 1953	July 1953
Cockade	July 1950	November 1950
	March 1951	August 1951
	October 1951	December 1951
	January 1952	March 1952
	December 1952	February 1953
	April 1953	July 1953
Concord	September 1950	January 1951
	April 1951	May 1951
	August 1951	November 1951
	January 1952	April 1952
	July 1952	August 1952
	May 1953	July 1953
Comus	July 1950	August 1950
	January 1951	June 1951
	September 1951	December 1951
	May 1952	September 1952
	November 1952	February 1953
Consort	June 1950	April 1951
	June 1951	September 1951
	May 1952	August 1952
	November 1952	February 1953
	March 1953	May 1953

Constance	October 1950	March 1951
	June 1951	July 1951
	November 1951	February 1952
	June 1952	December 1952
Cossack	June 1950	October 1951
	February 1952	May 1952
	July 1952	September 1952
	May 1953	July 1953
Black Swan	June 1950	August 1950
	February 1951	June 1951
	September 1951	November 1951
Alacrity	June 1950	August 1950
	February 1951	June 1951
	December 1951	February 1952
Amethyst	February 1951	June 1951
	September 1951	January 1952
	April 1952	June 1952
Crane	March 1952	June 1952
	August 1952	September 1952
	November 1952	July 1953
Hart	June 1950	August 1950
	February 1951	March 1951
Modeste	April 1953	July 1953
Opossum	November 1952	April 1953
Sparrow	December 1952	February 1953
	April 1953	June 1953
Cardigan Bay	November 1950	January 1951
	June 1951	September 1951
	January 1952	April 1952
	June 1952	September 1952
	January 1953	July 1953

Morecambe Bay	October 1950	January 1951
	June 1951	September 1951
	March 1952	May 1952
	August 1952	November 1952
	March 1953	July 1953
Mounts Bay	August 1950	November 1950
	December 1950	January 1951
	June 1951	September 1951
	December 1951	April 1952
	June 1952	November 1952
	March 1953	June 1953
St Brides Bay	December 1950	January 1951
	August 1951	December 1951
	July 1952	October 1952
	April 1953	June 1953
Whitesand Bay	August 1950	December 1950
	June 1951	July 1951
	October 1951	February 1952
	April 1952	July 1952
	February 1953	July 1953

INDEX

161

INDEX OF UNITED STATES NAVY
AND REPUBLIC OF KOREA VESSELS IN THE TEXT OF WCSG